The Essentials of Reading

College and Career/Second Edition

Pamela W. Petty
Daniel J. Super
Jessica Bryant

Kendall Hunt
publishing company

Cover image © Shutterstock, Inc.

Kendall Hunt
p u b l i s h i n g   c o m p a n y

www.kendallhunt.com
Send all inquiries to:
4050 Westmark Drive
Dubuque, IA   52004-1840

Copyright © 2013, 2016 by Pamela W. Petty, Daniel J. Super, and Jessica Bryant

ISBN 978-1-4652-9715-0

Printed in the United States of America

Dedication

This book is dedicated to my husband, Sam, to our son, Matt, our daughter, Lindsey and her husband, T.J., and to three very important people who bookend my life: my mother Shelby Jean White, who is always my biggest fan, my precious granddaughter, Ella Kaye Dixon, and my incredible grandson, Wyatt Andrew Dixon. You all make me laugh.

Dr. Pamela W. Petty, Ed.D.

This book is dedicated to my family, who not only put up with me, but for some reason have the unwavering belief that I can do anything.

Dr. Daniel Super, Ed.D.

This book is dedicated to my son, Erwin, a good reader and to my husband, Erwin Sr., who was patient enough for me to write this book. This book is also dedicated to my parents, who instilled in me the love of reading. Finally, this book is dedicated to all the high school and college students who are struggling to read. May you find this book an oasis in the desert.

Dr. Jessica Bryant, Ed.D.

About the Authors

Dr. Pamela Petty is a Professor of Literacy at Western Kentucky University in Bowling Green, Kentucky. She is the co-director of the WKU Center for Literacy and is the author and director of numerous grants and awards. She serves on several state and national committees. Her professional interests and research agendas include P-12 literacy preparation for college  and career readiness, postsecondary efforts to support and enhance student literacy, and the impacts of state and national educational initiatives/mandates on higher education.

Dr. Daniel Super is a Clinical Assistant Professor in the School of Teacher Education at Western Kentucky University. As the co-director of the WKU Center for Literacy, he works with hundreds of teachers and students every year in the areas of literacy and college readiness.

Dr. Jessica Bryant is Professor and Reading Coordinator in the Department of English & Theatre at Eastern Kentucky University. Since earning a doctoral degree in Education, with a focus in cultural literacy from the University of Kentucky, she has taught reading and writing courses at EKU for 20 years. She teaches developmental students, college readiness students, and graduate students.

Jessica works on a number of committees at EKU, has served on several college readiness committees with the Council on Postsecondary Education, and has contributed to developing college readiness standards for the state. She is the author of several articles on cultural literacy.

Contents

Table of Contents by Common Core Standards: Anchor Standards for College and Career Readiness, English/Language Arts

Key Ideas and Details	Chapter	Strategy
CCSS.ELA-Literacy.CCRA.R.2 Determine central ideas or themes of a text and analyze their development; summarize the key supporting details and ideas.	2. I feel like I am a responsible person—I can keep a dog and a plant alive at the same time. What else do responsible people do that would help me as an adult?	Character Trait Analysis with Evidence
	8. How do I put the "active" in active reading?	Reduce and Produce
	10. How can I read so that I can remember what I read?	You Be the Professor
	12. How can I possibly know what the author is thinking or what he wants me to know?	Text Annotation, Synthesis of Two Sources
	13. We get reading assignments of 50 to 60 pages in multiple courses per week. How can I possibly get through that much reading when I have no time?	Skimming, Scanning, and Trackers
	15. My books are full of charts, graphs, callouts, and pictures with captions. It makes it go faster if I skip those and just read the paragraphs. Is that a good strategy?	Text to Graphic
	19. I highlight the important parts. Isn't that good enough?	Summarizing
CCSS.ELA-Literacy.CCRA.R.3 Analyze how and why individuals, events, or ideas develop and interact over the course of a text.	2. I feel like I am a responsible person—I can keep a dog and a plant alive at the same time. What else do responsible people do that would help me as an adult?	Character Trait Analysis with Evidence
	14. How is the way I read a novel different than the way I read a textbook?	Visualization

Table of Contents by Common Core Standards: Anchor Standards for College and Career Readiness, English/Language Arts (continued)

Key Ideas and Details	Chapter	Strategy
CCSS.ELA-Literacy.CCRA.R.5 Analyze the structure of texts, including how specific sentences, paragraphs, and larger portions of the text (e.g., a section, chapter, scene, or stanza) relate to each other and the whole.	1. What if I am an admitted lazy person? Is there any fix for lazy?	Mind Mapping
	11. How can something I read mean more than it says?	QAR
	13. We get reading assignments of 50 to 60 pages in multiple courses per week. How can I possibly get through that much reading when I have no time?	Skimming, Scanning, and Trackers
	17. How can I make myself be interested in what I read?	Dialectical Notes
CCSS.ELA-Literacy.CCRA.R.6 Assess how point of view or purpose shapes the content and style of a text.	11. How can something I read mean more than it says?	QAR
Integration of Knowledge and Ideas		
CCSS.ELA-Literacy.CCRA.R.7 Integrate and evaluate content presented in diverse media and formats, including visually and quantitatively, as well as in words.	11. How can something I read mean more than it says?	QAR
	18. How can I take notes and listen at the same time?	Note-Taking from Multiple Sources
	20. I want to sound intelligent when I talk in class. How do I do that?	Text Coding

Table of Contents by Common Core Standards: Anchor Standards for College and Career Readiness, English/Language Arts (continued)

Key Ideas and Details		Chapter	Strategy
Range of Reading and Level of Text Complexity			
CCSS.ELA-Literacy.CCRA.R.10 Read and comprehend complex literary and informational texts independently and proficiently.		9. What does setting a purpose for reading have to do with comprehension?	Setting a Purpose
		10. How can I read so that I can remember what I read?	You Be the Professor
		13. We get reading assignments of 50 to 60 pages in multiple courses per week. How can I possibly get through that much reading when I have no time?	Skimming, Scanning, and Trackers

Table of Contents by Strategies, Passages, and Common Core Standards

	Question Submitted	Strategy Used	Standards Aligned
1	What if I am an admitted lazy person? Is there any fix for lazy?	Mind Mapping	CCSS.ELA-Literacy.CCRA.R.8 Delineate and evaluate the argument and specific claims in a text, including the validity of the reasoning as well as the relevance and sufficiency of the evidence. CCSS.ELA-Literacy.CCRA.R.5 Analyze the structure of texts, including how specific sentences, paragraphs, and larger portions of the text (e.g., a section, chapter, scene, or stanza) relate to each other and the whole.
2	I feel like I am a responsible person—I can keep a dog and a plant alive at the same time. What else do responsible people do that would help me as an adult?	Character Trait Analysis with Evidence	CCSS.ELA-Literacy.CCRA.R.1 Read closely to determine what the text says explicitly and to make logical inferences from it; cite specific textual evidence when writing or speaking to support conclusions drawn from the text. CCSS.ELA-Literacy.CCRA.R.2 Determine central ideas or themes of a text and analyze their development; summarize the key supporting details and ideas. CCSS.ELA-Literacy.CCRA.R.3 Analyze how and why individuals, events, or ideas develop and interact over the course of a text. CCSS.ELA-Literacy.CCRA.R.4 Interpret words and phrases as they are used in a text, including determining technical, connotative, and figurative meanings, and analyze how specific word choices shape meaning or tone.

	Question Submitted	Strategy Used	Standards Aligned
3	I am living like a poverty-stricken college student and wonder if this will ever end. Is a college degree worth it?	Synthesize, Reflect, and "Teach"	CCSS.ELA-Literacy.CCRA.R.8 Delineate and evaluate the argument and specific claims in a text, including the validity of the reasoning as well as the relevance and sufficiency of the evidence.
4	Why should I read if my grades in the course don't depend on the reading but on taking notes and learning the PowerPoint slides?	Personal Response to Reading	CCSS.ELA-Literacy.CCRA.R.1 Read closely to determine what the text says explicitly and to make logical inferences from it; cite specific textual evidence when writing or speaking to support conclusions drawn from the text.
5	How do I set up a study situation where I can actually get some work done?	Cornell Notes	CCSS.ELA-Literacy.CCRA.R.1 Read closely to determine what the text says explicitly and to make logical inferences from it; cite specific textual evidence when writing or speaking to support conclusions drawn from the text.
6	I feel like I missed some basics in reading. What does every student, parent, and adult need to know about reading?	Word Recognition Skills and Practice	

Table of Contents by Strategies, Passages, and Common Core Standards (continued)

	Question Submitted	Strategy Used	Standards Aligned
7	How can I know what the important parts are of what I am reading?	SQ3R (Covert)	CCSS.ELA-Literacy.CCRA.R.1 Read closely to determine what the text says explicitly and to make logical inferences from it; cite specific textual evidence when writing or speaking to support conclusions drawn from the text.
8	How do I put the "active" in active reading?	Reduce and Produce	CCSS.ELA-Literacy.CCRA.R.1 Read closely to determine what the text says explicitly and to make logical inferences from it; cite specific textual evidence when writing or speaking to support conclusions drawn from the text. CCSS.ELA-Literacy.CCRA.R.2 Determine central ideas or themes of a text and analyze their development; summarize the key supporting details and ideas. CCSS.ELA-Literacy.CCRA.R.8 Delineate and evaluate the argument and specific claims in a text, including the validity of the reasoning as well as the relevance and sufficiency of the evidence.
9	What does setting a "purpose for reading" have to do with comprehension?	Setting a Purpose	CCSS.ELA-Literacy.CCRA.R.10 Read and comprehend complex literary and informational texts independently and proficiently.
10	How can I read so that I can remember what I read?	You Be the Professor	CCSS.ELA-Literacy.CCRA.R.2 Determine central ideas or themes of a text and analyze their development; summarize the key supporting details and ideas. CCSS.ELA-Literacy.CCRA.R.10 Read and comprehend complex literary and informational texts independently and proficiently.

	Question Submitted	Strategy Used	Standards Aligned
11	How can something I read mean more than it says?	QAR	CCSS.ELA-Literacy.CCRA.R.4 Interpret words and phrases as they are used in a text, including determining technical, connotative, and figurative meanings, and analyze how specific word choices shape meaning or tone. CCSS.ELA-Literacy.CCRA.R.5 Analyze the structure of texts, including how specific sentences, paragraphs, and larger portions of the text (e.g., a section, chapter, scene, or stanza) relate to each other and the whole. CCSS.ELA-Literacy.CCRA.R.6 Assess how point of view or purpose shapes the content and style of a text. CCSS.ELA-Literacy.CCRA.R.7 Integrate and evaluate content presented in diverse media and formats, including visually and quantitatively, as well as in words.
12	How can I possibly know what the author is thinking or wants me to know?	Text Annotation, Synthesis of Two Sources	CCSS.ELA-Literacy.CCRA.R.2 Determine central ideas or themes of a text and analyze their development; summarize the key supporting details and ideas. CCSS.ELA-Literacy.CCRA.R.9 Analyze how two or more texts address similar themes or topics in order to build knowledge or to compare the approaches the authors take.
13	We get reading assignments of 50 to 60 pages in multiple courses per week. How can I possibly get through that much reading when I have no time?	Skimming, Scanning, and Trackers	CCSS.ELA-Literacy.CCRA.R.2 Determine central ideas or themes of a text and analyze their development; summarize the key supporting details and ideas. CCSS.ELA-Literacy.CCRA.R.5 Analyze the structure of texts, including how specific sentences, paragraphs, and larger portions of the text (e.g., a section, chapter, scene, or stanza) relate to each other and the whole. CCSS.ELA-Literacy.CCRA.R.10 Read and comprehend complex literary and informational texts independently and proficiently.

Table of Contents by Strategies, Passages, and Common Core Standards *(continued)*

	Question Submitted	Strategy Used	Standards Aligned
14	How is the way I read a novel different than the way I read a textbook?	Visualization	CCSS.ELA-Literacy.CCRA.R.3 Analyze how and why individuals, events, or ideas develop and interact over the course of a text. CCSS.ELA-Literacy.CCRA.R.4 Interpret words and phrases as they are used in a text, including determining technical, connotative, and figurative meanings, and analyze how specific word choices shape meaning or tone.
15	My books are full of charts, graphs, callouts, and pictures with captions. It makes it go faster if I skip those and just read the paragraphs. Is that a good strategy?	Text to Graphic	CCSS.ELA-Literacy.CCRA.R.1 Read closely to determine what the text says explicitly and to make logical inferences from it; cite specific textual evidence when writing or speaking to support conclusions drawn from the text. CCSS.ELA-Literacy.CCRA.R.2 Determine central ideas or themes of a text and analyze their development; summarize the key supporting details and ideas.
16	How do I find pleasure in reading when I hate it so much?	Character Profiling	CCSS.ELA-Literacy.CCRA.R.1 Read closely to determine what the text says explicitly and to make logical inferences from it; cite specific textual evidence when writing or speaking to support conclusions drawn from the text. CCSS.ELA-Literacy.CCRA.R.4 Interpret words and phrases as they are used in a text, including determining technical, connotative, and figurative meanings, and analyze how specific word choices shape meaning or tone.

	Question Submitted	Strategy Used	Standards Aligned
17	How can I make myself be interested in what I read?	Dialectical Notes	CCSS.ELA-Literacy.CCRA.R.4 Interpret words and phrases as they are used in a text, including determining technical, connotative, and figurative meanings, and analyze how specific word choices shape meaning or tone. CCSS.ELA-Literacy.CCRA.R.5 Analyze the structure of texts, including how specific sentences, paragraphs, and larger portions of the text (e.g., a section, chapter, scene, or stanza) relate to each other and the whole.
18	How can I take notes and listen at the same time?	Note-Taking from Multiple Sources	CCSS.ELA-Literacy.CCRA.R.7 Integrate and evaluate content presented in diverse media and formats, including visually and quantitatively, as well as in words. CCSS.ELA-Literacy.CCRA.R.8 Delineate and evaluate the argument and specific claims in a text, including the validity of the reasoning as well as the relevance and sufficiency of the evidence. CCSS.ELA-Literacy.CCRA.R.9 Analyze how two or more texts address similar themes or topics in order to build knowledge or to compare the approaches the authors take.
19	I highlight the important parts when I read. Isn't that good enough?	Summarizing	CCSS.ELA-Literacy.CCRA.R.2 Determine central ideas or themes of a text and analyze their development; summarize the key supporting details and ideas.

Table of Contents by Strategies, Passages, and Common Core Standards *(continued)*

	Question Submitted	Strategy Used	Standards Aligned
20	I want to sound intelligent when I talk in class. How do I do that?	Text Coding	CCSS.ELA-Literacy.CCRA.R.7 Integrate and evaluate content presented in diverse media and formats, including visually and quantitatively, as well as in words. CCSS.ELA-Literacy.CCRA.R.8 Delineate and evaluate the argument and specific claims in a text, including the validity of the reasoning as well as the relevance and sufficiency of the evidence. CCSS.ELA-Literacy.CCRA.R.9 Analyze how two or more texts address similar themes or topics in order to build knowledge or to compare the approaches the authors take.
21	Why is it that I can learn specific science words or words in other disciplines, but I am constantly running into big words I don't know when I just read?	Cracking the Vocab Code	CCSS.ELA-Literacy.CCRA.R.4 Interpret words and phrases as they are used in a text, including determining technical, connotative, and figurative meanings, and analyze how specific word choices shape meaning or tone.
22	Crossword? You mean "crossNERD?" How in the world could playing word games make me more literate?	Making Riddles	CCSS.ELA-Literacy.CCRA.R.4 Interpret words and phrases as they are used in a text, including determining technical, connotative, and figurative meanings, and analyze how specific word choices shape meaning or tone.

	Question Submitted	Strategy Used	Standards Aligned
23	A synonym, an antonym, and a homonym all walk into a bar . . . nah, not really. However, how can I keep all of these things straight and how can they help me have a better command of language?	Synonym Swap	CCSS.ELA-Literacy.CCRA.R.4 Interpret words and phrases as they are used in a text, including determining technical, connotative, and figurative meanings, and analyze how specific word choices shape meaning or tone.

So Why This Book?

This book offers instructors, college students, senior-level high school students, and adult learners with opportunities to increase their effectiveness with using print for learning. All aspects of the reading processes are addressed with particular emphasis on the skills and strategies that align with the Common Core Standards for English Language Arts. The authors divided the book into five parts. Part I addresses habits, behaviors, and mindsets that affect success. Part II provides information and practice with strategy-based reading comprehension. Part III moves through some of the barriers to active reading. Part IV focuses on the many different ways readers can collect information from print to enhance content learning. Part V speaks to the acquisition and importance of a strong academic vocabulary.

Each chapter is posed as a question that a reader might ask. The authors have provided responses to those questions as well as paired each with a strategy that aligns with one or more of the College and Career Anchor Standards of the Common Core Standards for English/Language Arts. Additionally, opportunities are provided within the book to apply those strategies with reading passages.

This book could be used:

- As the core reading textbook for a developmental, remedial, or supplemental reading course at the postsecondary level;

- As the core reading textbook for a high school reading transition to college course;

- In an adult education institution with learners working toward increasing their proficiency in reading for the GED;

- By individuals seeking to proactively prepare themselves for the rigors of reading in college and career.

The chapters in this book are aligned with the College and Career Anchor Standards of the Common Core Standards for English/Language Arts located at the following site www.commoncore.org (see English Language Arts Standards) and are listed next:

Key Ideas and Details

- **CCSS.ELA-Literacy.CCRA.R.1** Read closely to determine what the text says explicitly and to make logical inferences from it; cite specific textual evidence when writing or speaking to support conclusions drawn from the text.

- **CCSS.ELA-Literacy.CCRA.R.2** Determine central ideas or themes of a text and analyze their development; summarize the key supporting details and ideas.

- **CCSS.ELA-Literacy.CCRA.R.3** Analyze how and why individuals, events, or ideas develop and interact over the course of a text.

Craft and Structure

- **CCSS.ELA-Literacy.CCRA.R.4** Interpret words and phrases as they are used in a text, including determining technical, connotative, and figurative meanings, and analyze how specific word choices shape meaning or tone.

- **CCSS.ELA-Literacy.CCRA.R.5** Analyze the structure of texts, including how specific sentences, paragraphs, and larger portions of the text (e.g., a section, chapter, scene, or stanza) relate to each other and the whole.

- **CCSS.ELA-Literacy.CCRA.R.6** Assess how point of view or purpose shapes the content and style of a text.

Integration of Knowledge and Ideas

- **CCSS.ELA-Literacy.CCRA.R.7** Integrate and evaluate content presented in diverse media and formats, including visually and quantitatively, as well as in words.

- **CCSS.ELA-Literacy.CCRA.R.8** Delineate and evaluate the argument and specific claims in a text, including the validity of the reasoning as well as the relevance and sufficiency of the evidence.

- **CCSS.ELA-Literacy.CCRA.R.9** Analyze how two or more texts address similar themes or topics in order to build knowledge or to compare the approaches the authors take.

Range of Reading and Level of Text Complexity

- **CCSS.ELA-Literacy.CCRA.R.10** Read and comprehend complex literary and informational texts independently and proficiently.

To the student:

Why should you read this book when you have so many other choices and assignments? The answer lies in the research. There is an alarming problem in this country in terms of students enrolling in a postsecondary institution (that means a college or university) and failing to graduate. For many of these students, failure occurs because they are unprepared or underprepared for the rigors of such an environment. However, even for those students who come to college prepared, they are still *inexperienced.* As they enter this new arena, most students have not yet refined the skills nor the mindset required to be successful.

In this book, you will find the answers to questions that are all too common among your peers who have blazed this trail before you. The focus of these answers is to first help you understand the power of character, responsibility, and work ethic. From there, if you have the mindset to succeed, the following chapters aim to guide you through the labyrinth of reading related requirements you will encounter as you pursue your degree. There is no single skill more important to success in academia than the ability to learn from print. Together, with the right attitude and personal integrity, your chances of graduating will increase exponentially. All learning, no matter the content or course, is made more efficient and permanent if the learner possesses the skills outlined in this book.

Oh yeah, and it's also not dry and wicked boring.

Preface

The Essentials of Reading: College and Career is a textbook and guide appropriate for postsecondary students and other adults who are interested in increasing their effectiveness in reading and using print for learning. The book addresses 23 of the most commonly asked questions by students who are entering college, technical schools, or the workplace regarding their learning habits, reading comprehension, learning from print, study skills such as note-taking, and growing strong academic vocabularies. Students are encouraged to use authentic materials (textbooks and readings from courses they are currently taking) as opportunities to apply strategies presented in this book. Emphasis is placed on developing higher-level analysis of complex text including vocabulary and strategic approaches to aid students in developing deep comprehension. Key experiences include exploration of and practice with a variety of strategies for gaining meaning from print and the study skills that college students need to be successful. Students will develop self-awareness of their reading capabilities as they grow as efficient and flexible readers.

Research Base

Many college students across the United States find themselves surprised that ACT and other reading assessment scores indicate that they are not ready for the rigors of college reading when they graduate from high school. While universities are working quickly to put intervention courses in place that address students' literacy needs to increase their comprehension and vocabulary levels, and ensure they are successful in their required college courses, students are not as quick to understand or appreciate the need for taking an extra course that focuses exclusively on growing reading skills and strategies. One disconnect seems to stem from the lack of appreciation students have for how vital strong comprehension and vocabulary skills are for success in all their college courses. Cox, Friesner, and Khayum (2003) cite several studies that emphasize the connection between underprepared students, retention, graduation rates and the effectiveness of reading skills courses. They also present empirical evidence on the effectiveness of reading skills courses offered at a four-year Midwest university, reporting that "students who enter college underprepared to read at the college level and who take and pass a reading skills course experience significantly greater success in college over the long term compared to similarly underprepared students who either do not take, or do not pass, such a course" (p. 189).

Likewise, several research-based and effective nontraditional intervention courses are represented in the literature, leaders in the field still push for more innovation in course design and delivery. Newly custom-designed initiatives could be crafted more specifically to fit the specific student populations, more acutely meeting student needs, and enhancing retention and graduation. The trend is for courses that are more "student or learning-centered" rather than "remedial" or developmental in nature (Flippo & Caverly, 2009, p. 371). Cognitive-based models should replace the stigma-charged and outdated deficiency models that often do not improve underprepared students' skill and strategy development or do not improve dropout and graduation rates (Gourgey, 1999; Mt. San Antonio, 2008; Flippo & Caverly, 2009; Bohr, 1994; Adelman, 1996; Maxwell, 1997). The best designed courses include learning experiences where students use cognitive-based models to learn about how the brain functions with language and learning. Additionally, strong literacy courses ask students to be metacognitive as they set personal literacy goals and develop personal success plans that extend beyond the scope of the reading course. Both of these types of learning experiences are reflected in the September 29, 2009 release of CCSSO's Career and College Readiness Standards for Reading, Writing, Speaking and Listening, is included with the following notation:

> To be college and career ready, students must engage in research and present their findings in writing and orally, in print and online. The ability to conduct research independently and effectively plays a fundamental role in gaining knowledge and insight in college and the workplace (http://www.corestandards.org/ELA-Literacy/CCRA).

Students need to be in constant connectivity in engaged, inquiry-based, learning communities (Leu and Kinzer, 2000). It is essential that different learning modules include options for group learning sessions allowing for instruction couched within social interactions, trust-building frameworks, and electronic communications between learning sessions. Simpson, Stahl, and Francis (2004) indicate that reading intervention courses must ensure that students know when, why, and how to apply any new strategy; students must have time to apply new strategies; strategy instruction must be content embedded; and students must be metacognitive in their reflection and evaluation of their own learning.

Furthermore, choice is another aspect of program planning that should be considered. Wink (2005) is one of many researchers who indicate that students need to take control over their own learning. Providing choice is one way to honor students as independent learners by allowing them to make decisions about what they want to learn and how they want to learn.

Two things need to come together for college freshmen to quickly become independent in their reading skills and strategies. First, reading and literacy courses must be developed that are sound in research-based curricula, consider students' strengths and weaknesses, and provide skills and strategy instruction for reading comprehension of complex text. Additionally, these courses must help students understand how to learn new words and grow their academic vocabularies. These courses need to allow students to have multiple learning experiences as they practice the new skills and strategies, receiving feedback, redirection, and validation of growth. Secondly, students must want to enhance their literacy skills. No course, regardless of rigor and quality, will impact students' levels of literacy unless students value the role of reading in learning and decide to take responsibility for their own learning and growth as they fully participate in the required course objectives.

Determinants of Success in College

Any resource or initiative to address student learning has to take into account characteristics that make up the complete learning "package" that is required of each student to be successful at the university level. Nelson (1998) and Yaworski, Weber, and Ibrahim, (2000) identified qualities or traits that are common among successful university students. Reading comprehension and study skills intervention courses or initiatives need also to include emphasis on each aspect of success as illustrated in Figure 1.

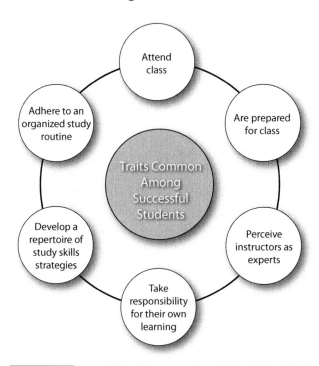

Figure 1

While the six characteristics listed above are common to all successful university students, underprepared students face additional challenges and therefore need to reach more levels of success than their more prepared peers. The first big obstacle to overcome is acknowledgment of needing assistance, followed closely by asking for assistance. "College students who are least prepared academically are least likely to seek out or attend academic support services offered to them" (Hodges & White, 2001 in Flippo & Caverly, 2009).

References

Adelman, C. (1996). *Point of view: The truth about remedial work: It's more complex than windy rhetoric and simple solutions suggest.* Chronicle of Higher Education, 36.

Bohr, L. (1994). College classes that attract and generate good readers. *Journal of College Reading & Learning*, 26(2), 30–44.

Cox, S. R., Friesner, D. L., & Khayum, M. (2003). Do reading skills courses help underprepared readers achieve academic success in college? *Journal of Adolescent & Adult Literacy*, 33 (2), 170–196.

Flippo, R. F., & Caverly, D. C., (2009). *Handbook of college reading and study strategy research*, 2ed. New York: Routledge.

Gourgey, A. F. (1999). Teaching reading from a metacognitive perspective: Theory and classroom experiences. *Journal of College Reading & Learning*, 30 (1), 85–93.

Hodges, R., & White, W. G., (2001). Encouraging high-risk student participation in tutoring and supplemental instruction. Journal of Developmental Education, 24 (9), 2–4, 6–8, 10, 43. In Flippo, R. F. & Caverly, D. C., (2009). *Handbook of college reading and study strategy research*, 2ed. (p. 57). New York: Routledge.

Leu, D. J., & Kinzer, C. K., (2000). The convergence of literacy instruction with networked technologies for information and communication. *Reading Research Quarterly*, 35(1), 108–127.

Maxwell, M. (1997). *The dismal state of required developmental reading programs: Roots, causes and solutions.* (ERIC Document Reproduction Service No. ED415501).

Mt. San Antonio College (2008). *Learning assistance center reading philosophy.* Retrieved November 27, 2008, from http://www .mtsac.edu/lac/lac_reading.html

Nelson, R. (1998). Using a student performance framework to analyze success and failure. *Journal of College Reading and Learning*, 29, 82–89.

Simpson, M. L., Stahl, N. A., & Francis, M. A., (2004). Reading and learning strategies: Recommendations for the 21st century. *Journal of Developmental Education*, 28 (2), p. 2–4, 6, 8, 10–12, 14–15.

Wink, J., (2005). *Critical pedagogy: Notes from the real world* (3rd ed.). New York: Pearson Education.

Yaworski, J., Weber, R., & Ibrahim, N., (2000). What makes students succeed or fail?: The voices of developmental college students. *Journal of College Reading and Learning*, 30, 195–221.

Part 1

Habits, Behaviors, and Mindsets

What if I am an admitted lazy person? Is there any fix for lazy?

If you find this question relatable, then you've taken the first step to fixing your problem by realizing that you might have some lazy tendencies. You may already be thinking about taking a break, having read two whole sentences, but push through. You can do this! Look, that sentence was only four words compared to the seventeen word sentence before it—that's a bonus. Keep the momentum going for a while and you'll see that not only is there a fix for lazy, but you may also find out that you are not as lazy as you might think.

Let's begin by putting everything on the table. Don't worry, you won't have to pick everything up and put it away; this is a proverbial table. When you think about yourself as lazy, there must be specific reasons why you consider yourself to be so slothful. What are those reasons? Is it because you don't get your schoolwork finished? Maybe you are overweight or unhealthy due to lack of exercise. Is it because your house/dorm is always dirty? There are reasons you feel the way you do about yourself. Take the time to rank the top three causes of your opinion:

1. _____

2. _____

3. _____

If your inability to start and finish making a list is one of your reasons, it is understandable why the blanks have nothing listed. If not, well you should have written three things. Your list is probably not all that different from every other person who detailed the rankings of his/her lethargy. Your list probably goes something like this: Exercising, Cleaning the house, Doing homework, Getting out of bed early in the morning, Doing manual labor, Going to work (job), etc. Close enough? Probably so. Now, take the time to consider another ranking. List the top three activities in which you engage most often when you have the free time, money, resources, etc., to do so:

1. _____

2. _____

3. _____

Would you consider yourself lazy when it comes to performing the activities you recorded on your second list? What is the difference? It's probably fair to generalize the first list a bit by saying that those activities, for the most part, are not particularly enjoyable. Most of the time, you feel like you *have* to do these things. The second list, however, includes activities that you *choose* to complete. So, does it mean that because you procrastinate or altogether avoid engaging in the items on your first list you are lazy? Not necessarily. If, when you have the opportunities to do the things from list two, you jump at the chance, then you aren't particularly lazy—you are *undisciplined.* See the difference? Lazy isn't particularly easy to fix. Undisciplined, however—that is something that can be addressed.

So, how do you become disciplined? Well, you could move across the country to Fresno, Calif., to live with your crazy uncle who teaches you discipline by making you build fences, wax cars, and catch flies with chopsticks. Or, in the case that you aren't the Karate Kid and cannot rely on the prophetic teachings of Mr. Miyagi, you can change some things in your life to get you on the right path. First, let's start with the end in mind. If you truly want to change your tendency to avoid/delay taking part in an activity from your list, you must see that your current behaviors are not acceptable and that completing the activity is worthwhile. Believe that your arrival at a new state of efficiency is the best choice you can make for your productivity, then make the choice and stick with it.

Because it is very difficult to give theoretical examples, let's take a concrete problem that many students are plagued with and use it to illustrate how to introduce discipline to achieve the desired result. So, let's use homework (or any iteration of completing schoolwork) as a target for change. The first step is to decide that the best thing for you to do is to finish the work. You must value it and set it as a priority. Next you have to guard yourself from yourself. You are an admitted undisciplined person, remember? Every fiber of your being will try to interfere with your ability to accomplish this horrifying task. You have to realize that will be the case and prepare for the onslaught of self-destructive behaviors. How can you guard yourself from yourself? One very effective way to do this is to manipulate your environment. If you fall asleep as soon as you get horizontal, don't study on your bed. If you can't help but update yourself on the happenings in the world of Facebook and Twitter, stay away from an Internet device. If you can't help but surf profile pages on Myspace, get back into your time machine and leave 2006 where it belongs. The point is, you know what temptations rear their ugly heads when it's time to do schoolwork. Eliminate those temptations. Schedule a time and a place to read or study. Make sure that nothing can interfere with your plan. It's really hard to get on the Internet or make a phone call if you are in a room without the devices to do either—ask a prisoner.

Now that you've recognized that completing the schoolwork is a priority and you've successfully warded off as many distractions and temptations as possible, you can engage in whatever it is you must do. Congrats! You did some work. It feels good, huh? Actually, endorphins are released in your brain and the pleasure centers are active. Physiologically, when you accomplish your goal, you feel good. So now what do you do? The exact same thing. Again—and again. You have to turn your good decisions into a *habit.* This is going to take some time. There is no secret sequence, there is no late-night infomercial system that costs $19.95, and there is no pill you swallow once a day. To turn positive, disciplined decisions into habits, it takes time. However, eventually those choices you made because you decided it was the best thing for you to do become routines you engage in because it is *who you are.*

It's not that you're lazy. We are all lazy in areas that are low on our priority list. You just haven't made some behaviors a priority. When you do, it becomes much easier to fulfill your obligations. In the meantime, you aren't just changing your behaviors; you are changing the very fiber of your being. It feels pretty rewarding to look back at that first list you made and cross off an item—not because you solved a *problem,* but because you fixed *yourself.*

Before you can make the necessary adjustments to your priority list, you first need to get an idea of how you are spending your time. It's not always as simple as sleeping 8 hours, working 8 hours, and having 8 hours of free time. There are a lot of pesky little time suckers that can ultimately cause you to lose control of the day. Take just a few minutes from your schoolwork category to complete the following activity:

How Do I Spend My Day?

Be general in your estimations. There is no need to use a stopwatch to time yourself tying your shoes. The purpose is to paint a broad picture of how and where you spend most of your time and to identify the leaks.

Time spent (in minutes) engaging in each of the following per day:

_____In class

_____Studying/doing homework

_____Sleeping

_____Exercising/playing sports

_____Working (internship/volunteering)

_____Family commitments (don't forget to call Mom)

_____Personal care/getting ready (like showering . . . remember this is per *day*, not per week)

_____Meal preparation/eating/cleanup

_____Transportation (to school, work, grocery, etc.)

_____Media (TV, video games, Internet)

_____Phone (talking, texting, apps/Internet)

_____Socializing/entertainment

_____Dating/pursuing a date (easy on the body spray, fellas)

_____Other: _____

_____**Total**

Was your total less than 24 hours? If so, you should have even more time to devote to another category.

Was your total more than 24 hours? If so, you're going to have to make some changes somewhere. You might look into the Media, Phone, and Socializing categories . . .

After looking at the numbers that you put in the previous activity, you may be wondering why you still seem to fail to find the time to get the most important things done. Do you always find yourself making last-minute decisions to adjust one category to give you some emergency extra time in the Studying/doing homework category? Most of the time this comes in the form of forfeiting sleep time (pulling an all-nighter) or missing out on something you really wanted to do because you waited until the last minute to write a research paper. You are a classic victim of procrastination. We all know that when we put things off until later, we are procrastinating, right? What if you were committing procrastination even when you didn't know it? What if there was more than one type of procrastination?

In fact, according to Rory Vaden, author of the best-selling book *Take the Stairs,* there are three types of procrastination. The first is *classic.* You are well aware of this type. This is simply putting off what you should be doing until a later time. This is certainly common, but you may very well be guilty of other forms of procrastination also. The next type is called *creative avoidance* (Vaden, 2012). Do you ever find yourself looking for quick and easy things to "get done" so you can "check them off your list"? Maybe you know that you should be writing that research paper, but instead you decide that you're going to clean the bathroom. At the end of the day, you were very productive. In fact, you are exhausted because you barely sat down to take a break. You weren't being lazy—you were busy. The problem is that you were not particularly effective where it counts the most. Your bathroom is clean, your baseboards are scrubbed, your spice cabinet is arranged in alphabetical order, and all of your socks have partners. But you still didn't write your research paper. You found reasons to do other things in order to effectively avoid the most important task. You procrastinated.

The third type of procrastination, according to Vaden, is *priority dilution* (2012). This occurs when, instead of writing your research paper, you begin filling your time with what is latest and loudest. This means that you answer the email that you just received. You answer the phone that is currently ringing. Just because something just came to your attention, doesn't necessarily mean it is more important than writing your paper. Again, your day is spent with "getting stuff done," but you have failed to write your paper. Procrastination got you again.

One way to help yourself prioritize is to force a decision regarding what is *imperative,* what is *important,* and what should be on the back burner. The fact is that just because you are doing *something,* it doesn't necessarily mean you are doing the *right* thing. If you don't proactively identify a pecking order, you will very likely fall

Plan the Week

Day of Week	Imperative	Important	If Time Allows	Keep in Mind
Monday				
Tuesday				
Wednesday				
Thursday				
Friday				

Day of Week	Imperative	Important	If Time Allows	Keep in Mind
Saturday				
Sunday				

victim to some form of procrastination. Every week, you should know what *must* be done, what is *important* to get done, and what can wait if time doesn't permit. Use the chart on pages 8 and 9 to help you keep it all straight.

Citation from this chapter is

Vaden, R. (2012). *Take the Stairs: 7 Steps to Achieving True Success.* New York: Perigee

Since we are talking about your mind and minding your business, let's try this chapter again with you representing the major thoughts (what the author wants you to know) and your comments/connections to those ideas. The Mind Mapping strategy is one that helps many people keep track of the main points and to make sense of how they are related.

The website http://www.mind-mapping.co.uk/ demonstrates the many applications of mind mapping for business and education. An example of a mind map of the Illumine program is drawn below:

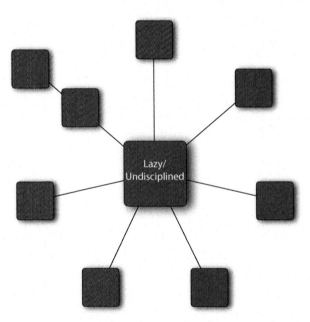

Grab your colored pens/markers and let's see how you can illustrate this chapter and add your own branching-out ideas—maybe a "notes-to-self-type-application." The words should go in the center of your mind map.

- **CCSS.ELA-Literacy.CCRA.R.8** Delineate and evaluate the argument and specific claims in a text, including the validity of the reasoning as well as the relevance and sufficiency of the evidence.
- **CCSS.ELA-Literacy.CCRA.R.5** Analyze the structure of texts, including how specific sentences, paragraphs, and larger portions of the text (e.g., a section, chapter, scene, or stanza) relate to each other and the whole.

I feel like I am a responsible person—I can keep a dog and a plant alive at the same time. What else do responsible people do that would help me as an adult?

Good news! A person, by the very virtue of asking such a question, is probably responsible in some way. The question seems to imply that you are indeed thinking about the future and what personal characteristics would be beneficial to you in your endeavors. That is, in fact, a responsible concern to have. Good for you. Look at you, all responsible and stuff. But having one responsible thought does not constitute a responsible personality. No, indeed, there are more things to consider. So before you get all high and mighty, you may need to pursue the answer to this question a bit more thoroughly. After all, it would be the responsible thing to do.

What it means to truly be a responsible person changes as you grow older. Remember how hard it was to be a kid? Maybe you had to make your bed and clean your room. You may have even had to feed your pet. You had to complete your homework and brush your teeth. That's pretty much it. Being a responsible kid may have felt like you had the weight of the world on your shoulders at the time, but now—not so much. As you continued to grow, so did the list of things for which you were responsible. You might have had a part time job or played a sport. You even had the responsibility to obey the rules of the road when you finally got your driver's license. You still had to brush your teeth and do your homework, but now some-one added "not killing pedestrians" to your list of chores. How exhausting. Maybe that is why you could never stay awake in Biology class.

Now that you are progressing into adulthood, you are about to fall into the proverbial ocean of responsibility. The time when you "step out into the *real world*" is one of the biggest changes you will ever encounter in your life. Many people aren't ready for it. We all know that guy who is "taking a break to figure out where to go next" or is "in between places right now." He is effectively attempting to call a time-out right in the middle of the race. Since life doesn't really work that way, instead of being awarded the time-out, he is really just sitting idly while everything else passes him at breakneck speed. Think of a stalled car at a NASCAR race—only the spectators are all wearing shirts. The point is that if you aren't ready for the incredible amplification of responsibility when the time comes, you will most likely fall behind and will be playing catch-up for a long time.

One thing that every responsible person realizes at some point or another is that he/she is an important piece in a variety of systems. When you were a kid, your responsibilities played a role in the functioning of your family's life as well as your school. If you didn't pick up your toys, who did? If you didn't brush your teeth, leading to a cavity and a trip to the dentist, who paid that bill? If you didn't do well on those state tests at the end of the school year, who got in trouble? The same goes for when you grew a bit older and got a job. If you didn't show up to work, did the place just shut down? Someone had to cover for you. When you have a responsibility, you must realize that *you* aren't the *only* person affected by your actions (or lack thereof). As an adult, you will have some very important roles to fulfill—roles that if you fail to give due attention, the consequences are significant. You will likely still be a son or daughter to your parents, as well as a brother or sister and aunt or uncle, however, these roles take less of your time than they have in the past. Now, as you enter your young adulthood, your responsibilities as a college student are consuming. You will have responsibilities as a tenant to pay rent, a roommate to help maintain a residence, and an employee (you have to get money from somewhere). Very soon you may have the pressure of being a husband or wife and then the honorable task of being a parent. All the while you will need to positively contribute to society and your community. You mustn't take any of these jobs lightly. Think about what happens to the other people involved in each paradigm when you fail to fulfill your responsibilities. The repercussions of a failure to adequately address each of these new duties are far more significant than if you forgot to make your bed when you were eleven. Now we're talking about careers and bills, marriages and kids, your country and the law. This is big kid stuff.

Responsibility is about pulling your own weight and not forcing any other person to do it for you. In our society, just so it can function, things have to be done and *people* have to do them. Seems obvious. However, when you really think about it, what happens when a person decides not to do his/her part? Was that part so nonessential that it was inconsequential? Usually not. Usually someone else has to make up for it. There is a sociological concept called *Social Loafing* that describes the mindset that many humans have when it comes to this subject. Essentially, social loafing is the idea that people in a group tend to not give their full effort because they know that someone else will pick up the slack. This has probably happened to you when a teacher assigns a group project. Everyone will receive the same grade, so almost inevitably, someone in the group will try to fade into the background while the other members of the group actually complete the project. Understanding that social loafing is a common human condition is an important step to being a responsible adult. Just because the job will eventually get done doesn't mean you should allow your co-workers to bear the brunt of the work while you play golf. Just because there are hundreds of millions of people and corporations contributing doesn't mean you should sneak out on paying your taxes. Someone else will have to pick up the slack and also, nobody will like you very much.

Recognizing biases is also a critical component to being a responsible adult. Just like social loafing, humans also have the tendency to revert to biases in thought. One such bias is *self-serving bias*. Because we want to look at ourselves in the best light possible, we often have a difficult time remembering accurately. More specifically, we tend to give ourselves credit when things go well and we tend to blame outside sources when things go poorly or we make mistakes. How many times have you heard your friends blame the teacher when they get a bad grade on a test or in a class? Do they also credit the teacher when they ace a test in another course? Usually not. Responsible adults recognize the tendency of holding a self-serving bias and can objectively look at the reasons for why they arrived at a negative result. Maybe they could have studied more, maybe they should have read the chapter again, maybe they shouldn't have skipped those Friday classes to go on a three day trip to see a Lil Wayne concert (and maybe they shouldn't have bothered to see a Lil Wayne concert at all—for any reason). If other people could get a good grade on the test, then *everyone* could have gotten a good grade. The blame cannot possibly be solely placed on the teacher. Responsible adults recognize that they cannot blame others for their own shortcomings *and* that they have to control their brains to avoid excusing those shortcomings through a self-serving bias type of thought.

Another biased way of thinking that we should be conscious of is *hindsight* bias. This occurs when we refuse to learn from our mistakes because we always want to be right. Since the only people who are always right are your mother and Judge Judy, we can safely assume that we are all wrong every once in a while. Hindsight bias tempts us to look back on our past and view ourselves as correct when we were wrong, as justified when we weren't, and as wise when we were ignorant. Responsible adults realize that making bad decisions and being wrong is a part of maturing and learning. However, if we always look back on our darkest days with a false ray of sunshine, we cannot learn anything.

Besides having a job, paying our bills, taking care of our family, paying our taxes, following the laws of the land, and learning from our mistakes, responsible people must also give constant attention to being informed and educated. Because we know that we are a vital piece of a much larger picture, we must make decisions every day that either contribute to or detract from our society as a whole. If we are not adequately informed to make such decisions, we are being grossly irresponsible when we *do* make those decisions. If you have an opinion or belief, you should be able to sufficiently present and defend the reasons for your stance. If, in fact, you cannot do either, if you can only fumble around with throwing insults and criticism at the opposition, you should probably just keep your mouth shut. Ignorance is dangerous. Ignorance fueled by a foolhardy opinion is terrifying. Responsible adults make efforts daily to be informed about the world, to be in a state of continual education, so that the decisions they make (or help to make) will be sound.

Responsibility isn't *just* about what we do. It's about how we think, how we learn, how we remember, and how we live. Recognizing the fact that these positions are always evolving and require constant attention is the only way any of us can continue to become more responsible. After all, being responsible for your own life affects the world around you just as much as it affects yourself.

- **CCSS.ELA-Literacy.CCRA.R.1** Read closely to determine what the text says explicitly and to make logical inferences from it; cite specific textual evidence when writing or speaking to support conclusions drawn from the text.

- **CCSS.ELA-Literacy.CCRA.R.2** Determine central ideas or themes of a text and analyze their development; summarize the key supporting details and ideas.

- **CCSS.ELA-Literacy.CCRA.R.3** Analyze how and why individuals, events, or ideas develop and interact over the course of a text.

- **CCSS.ELA-Literacy.CCRA.R.4** Interpret words and phrases as they are used in a text, including determining technical, connotative, and figurative meanings, and analyze how specific word choices shape meaning or tone.

Chapter 3

I am living like a poverty-stricken college student and wonder if this will ever end. Is a college degree worth it?

Nobody is interested in the anthropology club. Let's all be honest with each other. You have better things to do than meet for two and a half hours every other Thursday afternoon in a musty classroom on the other side of campus. Luckily for you, half of the people in the room feel the same way you do about the accommodations and the conversation. But you don't mind the façade. Your focus is pointed. You are here for one thing and one thing only—OK, two things if you count the cute girl in the corner wearing those no prescription glasses and her hair in a pony tail—but you came here for the pizza. If it turns into a date, great; maybe she'll buy. Thanks to the generous funding from the last will and testament of old man what's-his-name, the anthropology club provides free pizza and soft drinks at every meeting. The worst-case scenario is that you have to sit through the drudgery of your self-righteous peers' blabbering; the best-case scenario is that you'll walk away with the leftover half of the stuffed-crust Meat Mania that the vegetarians wouldn't touch. That should hold you over until the chess club meets on Monday afternoon.

Everybody loves a free meal, especially when your alternative is two packs of Ramen noodles and a glass of Kool-Aid. In college, it doesn't take long to scope out the easiest way to get free things. When you're broke, you become very sensitive to the giveaways. At least everyone you know is broke, too. Actually, it's kind of just part of the atmosphere; it's cool. Yeah, let's go with that—it's cool.

There are some parts about being a broke college student that aren't so cool. Like when you want to go out on a date with the cute girl you met at the anthropology club meeting and you realize that it's probably going to have to be a PB&J picnic or a call to mom and dad to bum some cash. A picnic could really score you points—it's very thoughtful. Except it is January and you'd be serving peanut butter and jelly with a side of frostbite. Love hurts. Sometimes being destitute means that you don't do laundry for a few weeks (maybe that has nothing to do with money) or that you walk instead of using the gas in your car. Now that you think about it, it's really not very cool to arm wrestle your roommate over the two quarters you found in the couch cushion. You should be the bigger man and just let him have the change, but the truth is that he is the bigger man—so he took it anyway.

This new world of poverty is not what you are used to. When you go back home for the weekend, your parents' pantry is like an oasis of snacks. Your mom sends you back with three containers of leftovers that you will guard with your life from your roommate and your dad slips you $40 as you hug goodbye. Yeah, living on your own in college is a lot different than being at your parents' house. Your parents are so comfortable. They seem to buy whatever they need or want and can still give you money. Just how does that happen? Maybe that's something you can think about during the three-hour drive back to campus in the car your parents bought for you when you were 16. Oh, look—a full tank of gas! You'd better remember to thank your dad for that next time you talk to him.

One date later with Ms. Anthropology, your $40 is gone thanks to the concession prices at the movie theater. You thought that there was no way she could eat a large popcorn, besides, could she not see that it cost $9? Oh well, love hurts. You think to yourself, "Am I ever going to be like my parents? Will I ever be anything but a broke college student?" The answer is (drum roll) . . . it depends. Anticlimactic? Sure it is. The decisions that you make in the next few years will determine the answer. Scary? Sure it is.

Before you get too nervous thinking about your future, reassure yourself of a few things. First, you've already done well enough in high school to get into college. Second, you are actually thinking about how important your future is and it makes you nervous. You're off to a good start, but from this point forward nothing will be given to you. You will have to work harder than you've (likely) ever worked on anything in your life to get through college. When it is finally all behind you and you hang your diploma on the wall of your new office at your new job, you will look back and be so proud of all of the work you did. But will it be worth it? Four, five, maybe six years sounds like a long time to be bound by such a burden. If you think that sounds like a long time to be stuck doing something that you don't particularly enjoy, how does 40 years sound? That's likely how long you'll be working in a job that you didn't exactly choose, that doesn't exactly pay well or offer retirement, and isn't exactly enjoyable. You could only quit in your mid to late sixties if social security is still solvent by then. I wouldn't exactly count on that. Take a look at the chart below about how beneficial a college degree can be when you enter the workforce:

2012 Unemployment Rate (%)	Education Attained	2012 Median Weekly Earnings (dollars)
2.5	Doctoral Degree	$1,624
2.1	Professional Degree	$1,735
3.5	Master's Degree	$1,300
4.5	Bachelor's Degree	$1,066
6.8	Associate Degree	$785
7.7	Some college, no degree	$727
8.3	High school graduate	$652
12.4	Less than high school diploma	$471
6.8	All Workers	$815

Source: Bureau of Labor Statistics, Current Population Survey.

There is a *huge* difference in the unemployment rate as well as the amount of money you will likely earn as you become more educated. These numbers are averages. Just because you get a degree does not necessarily guarantee that you will get a job or make this amount of money. There are many factors to consider. Not all degrees are created equally. You may be very philosophically inclined. You may wow your friends and classmates with your intellectually provoking questions and insights. However, unless you can find some toga-wearing, Greek-inspired, marble-office company that will pay you to be thoughtful, you should probably choose a major that will allow you to get hired. Or, maybe you think the numbers on the right column of this chart all look very appealing. Hey, when you are a broke college student, even $471 per week sounds like a lot of money. Before you get too excited about bringing home the proverbial bacon, you should also consider what you currently *pay* for. You see, it costs a lot of money to live—like a whole lot. Right now you may be responsible for your spending money, your gasoline, and your cell phone, but if somebody else is footing the bill for everything else it may be difficult to truly understand how expensive the world can be. To really get a flavor for the financial responsibilities of the real world, take the time to complete the following exercises:

Look again at the chart regarding how much money the average person makes per degree attainment. What do you want to "be" when you graduate again? Circle that level of degree and then calculate how much money you will make (gross) per month:

2012 Unemployment Rate (%)	Education Attained	2012 Median Weekly Earnings (dollars)
2.5	Doctoral Degree	$1,624
2.1	Professional Degree	$1,735
3.5	Master's Degree	$1,300
4.5	Bachelor's Degree	$1,066
6.8	Associate Degree	$785
7.7	Some college, no degree	$727
8.3	High school graduate	$652
12.4	Less than high school diploma	$471
6.8	All Workers	$815

_____/week × 4 weeks = _____

Figure A

For the sake of simplicity, let's just assume that your job offers retirement and insurance. Although this is going to seem like a huge blow to the ol' pocketbook, getting insurance and retirement through your employer is a huge savings compared to buying it on your own, so be thankful. Now calculate how much money you will lose from your paycheck every month by multiplying your gross amount by .67 to obtain your net income per month. Why .67? Well, you have to pay Uncle Sam, your insurance, and your retirement. All of that is typically about 33% of your check. If you multiply the gross number by .67, you get the amount of money that you can actually take home and put in your piggy bank every month. Don't put it all in there, because you have some bills to pay.

Use the following worksheet to estimate the monthly expense for each category:

Outgoing Bills Average/Month			
Utilities		**Necessities**	
Electricity	_____	Groceries	_____
Water	_____	Auto Insurance	_____
Trash Pickup	_____	Gasoline	_____
(Home Phone)	_____		
		Discretionary	
Conveniences		Clothing	_____
Cable TV	_____	Entertainment	_____
Internet	_____	Eating at a	
Cell Phone	_____	Restaurant	_____
		Potentially	
		Student Loan	_____
		Personal Debt	_____
		School Bills	_____
		Childcare	_____
		Savings	_____
Total Outgoing	_____		

Figure B

Breathe, now breathe. Calm down. Being a grown up is hard, but don't go dying on me. Did you have any money left over? If you didn't, you need to make an adjustment somewhere. You can go back to figure A and make more money (maybe get a second job at the Krispy Kreme) or get a higher degree to make more money or you might have to trim some fat from figure B. It's your choice really. What you cannot do is spend more money than you take in; only the government can do that.

If you did happen to have some cash left over (or if you made some adjustments), now you're ready for the next step. Yes, there is a next step. You may have noticed the absence of two common bills that must be paid every month. These are the variables—the big ones. These two payments are what separate the tiers in society. Your *home* and your *car.* You have to live somewhere and you must have a vehicle to drive you to work. All of the bills that you estimated to arrive at the monthly expenses for figure B were very common expenses. We don't think about rich people and say, "Oh girl, she's so rich, she has running water in her house!" When is the last time you described a very successful person as "having electricity"? Those are expenses that *everyone* pays. When you think of someone doing well for himself, you talk about where he lives or what he drives. It's not that your home and your car are inherently important in terms of social status or that you should even care about social status. The point is these are the variables. What type of home can you live in given your monthly expenses? What type of car can you drive? Finish the exercise by completing the final step.

Housing and Vehicle

Now that you know how much money it will take to pay for the things you need/want, where are you going to live? What vehicle will you drive to work?

Use Figure C

Using the Internet, find housing that you could reasonably afford. To give you some perspective, the following are expected mortgage payments based on a 30-year fixed loan with 4% APY interest rate:

$100,000 = $581.58

$125,000 = $726.98

$150,000 = $872.27

$175,000 = $1,017.77

$200,000 = $1,163.16

You will also need a vehicle to transport you from A to B. Most individuals/families have at least one car payment per month. Using the Internet, find a car/truck that you could reasonably afford. To give you some perspective, the following are expected monthly payments based on 6% sales tax and a 7.5% interest rate:

3 Year Loan	5 Year Loan
$5,000 = $164.86	$5,000 = $106.20
$10,000 = $329.73	$10,000 = $212.40
$15,000 = $494.59	$15,000 = $318.60
$20,000 = $659.45	$20,000 = $424.80
$25,000 = $824.31	$25,000 = $531.01

Makes you think, huh? Actually, it may even make your nose bleed or your ulcer flare up. It's scary. Living is hard work. The choices that you make during these college years will greatly influence *how* hard living will be from now on. Four or five years of sacrifice now—doing things in every class that you don't really want to do is *far* preferable to working in whatever dead-end job you can land, making whatever it is it will pay you, with no options of a better life for the next 40 plus years. However, nobody will make you be successful. That's really up to you.

This reading gave you a chance to read about something that is personal to you—your wallet/purse. You were likely interested and engaged throughout. However, you may be one of those folks who says they have trouble remembering what they read. What if you were asked to explain what you learned from this to someone else? That would set you up for the best learning possible: teaching. When you learn something well enough to teach it to someone else, you have all "hands on deck," so-to-speak, regarding your brain being engaged. The ultimate learning is preparation for and the actual act of teaching.

From the information you just read, what do you wish you would have already known? Why didn't someone already share this with you? If you wish that you'd have known before now, there are likely others who also need to know before it's too late. If you had the opportunity to talk to some students just a bit younger than you, what would you say? Prepare a one-page "presentation" handout for advising high school seniors and incoming freshmen on how to "stretch a dollar 'til it snaps!" You can use up to 25% of the information on your handout from the information you read here. The other 75% of the information on your one-pager should be advice and information from your own life. The following template will prompt you for information to include. You should use it as a pre-plan for your writing. You may structure the page you complete using any format you feel would best advertise your information. You should submit your pre-plan form with your completed one-pager. By engaging your mind in this type of activity, you allow yourself the additional opportunity to work with the information, put it in your own words, and then teach it to others. Now, you'll remember it.

> • **CCSS.ELA-Literacy.CCRA.R.8** Delineate and evaluate the argument and specific claims in a text, including the validity of the reasoning as well as the relevance and sufficiency of the evidence.

Pre-Planning for One-Pager

Goal:

One-page visual and text representation of your view of financial independence in college—25% max from textbook and 75% reflection of your own reality

---

| Summarize here what you learned from this reading: | Jot down a few words related to what you want to tell: |

What design idea do I have so that my one-pager is informative and will get the attention of my readers?

Consider any images that would make your one-pager more interesting.

Image © Vitaly Korovin, 2013. Used under license from Shutterstock, Inc.

Image © sgame, 2013. Used under license from Shutterstock, Inc.

Information From Reading	My Own Reality
Might include info on the "musts" all persons have to consider to live	Tell as much information as you are comfortable sharing
Other info	Think about things that high school seniors or college freshmen should consider
Other info	My own personal experiences
My ideas based on info in reading	Ways I know to "live cheap"
What I know about finances in general	What I know about finances in general
What I believe about my future income based on everything I know	Tips and advice from me—my own voice should be clear in this part

Why should I read if my grades in the course don't depend on the reading but on taking notes and learning the PowerPoint slides?

You remember how busy you felt while you were in high school? Those classes required far more work than the junior high courses you had mastered. By the time you added sports, dating (or time spent trying to get a date), driving, and a part-time job, you were one busy teenager. In fact, it was the busiest you had ever been in your life. Remember that? Actually, you probably long for those carefree days now that you've experienced the responsibilities of college life. Now that you are the keeper of your own schedule, you've likely realized that it is difficult to stay on top of the reading, the studying, and the writing—not to mention working, exercising, socializing, and at some point, sleeping. There just aren't enough hours in the day. Every week, if not every day, you run through a mental or physical checklist of "musts." For most of you, if the item on the list doesn't *have* to be done today, it probably won't get done today. Ah, college procrastination. If you have to prioritize your list like this every day just to survive, then there is no way you would do *extra* work, right? Where would it fit? To quote the scholar Sweet Brown, "ain't nobody got time for that!" Let's say your professor says, "Read Chapter 2 before next class." Before everyone packs their bags to leave, Little Miss Valedictorian in the front row asks, "Will this be on the test?" A collective silence sweeps the room as everyone pauses in mid-movement to hear the answer to such an important question. "Well, not per se," your professor answers, "I just thought you should be exposed to some of the information in the chapter." We all know what just happened. Only Suzie Brown Noser in the front row is going to read Chapter 2. The rest of the class made a mental check beside that box and has already moved on. But maybe there is a reason Ms. Brown Noser is such a know-it-all; maybe she's on to something.

The reasons you would give for failing to read the Chapter 2 assignment are that, one, obviously your time is very precious and you certainly do not want to misuse any of it by reading something you don't *have* to read; and two, you will never be tested over the material. It's a proverbial, "Why would I?" If you will not be held accountable, why would you *waste* your time reading a chapter? No time. Not for a grade. Got it. You win—or do you?

You probably already know that your excuses are misplaced and silly, but you're sticking to your guns. That's fair for now. We can address your bad habits in a few minutes, but first, how about a story? A professor at a university was tired of hearing the same excuse from his students as to why they couldn't possibly meet the expectations of his course. The students were overloaded. They simply did not have time to accomplish all of the tasks set forth by every professor. Besides that, they had jobs, families, significant others. They were an "active part of the student body." He was asking too much. In fact, he should probably lighten the load a bit. After a few semesters of hearing the same old thing, he decided to do a demonstration. With the help of a wagon, the professor hauled in an empty aquarium, three bags, and a gallon of water. He told the students that before class began he wanted to get their opinion on something. He sat the empty aquarium on the table in the front of the room. After opening one of the bags, he showed the students that it was full of baseballs. He said, "I am going to pour baseballs out of this bag into this aquarium until you tell me to stop." He began dumping them into the aquarium and it quickly began to fill up. A few students told him to stop once they reached the top. "Why am I stopping?" the professor asked. "Because the aquarium is full," a student replied. "There is no more room." After some back and forth, the class unanimously decided that the aquarium was completely full. The professor then opened a second bag. This bag contained marbles. He began pouring the marbles into the aquarium and they nestled their way into the crevices left by the stack of baseballs. The students began murmuring, understanding that they shouldn't have claimed the aquarium was full. "Now is it full?" the professor asked, as he finished pouring the marbles. "*Now* it's full," the class responded. So, the professor opened his third bag. This bag was full of BBs. A few of the students laughed out loud, realizing that they had again been too quick to judge the aquarium's capacity for holding spherical objects. The professor dumped the bag of BBs in with the rest of the contents and held up the empty bag. "Now it's full?" he asked, almost rhetorically. Nobody dared to answer this time. Their track record was not good at this point. Finally, he held up the gallon of water and began pouring until the level rose to the top of the aquarium. "Now it is full," he said. "There is absolutely nothing else that we can fit in this aquarium."

The truth is this: Humans will always find a way to do what they really want to do. We will make sacrifices and adjustments to allow ourselves to partake in the activities we really desire. It is all about prioritization. Try it. Look at how you spend your time. You will find that your list mirrors your priorities. Let's take some parallels from our professorial proverb (that's *alliteration*—look it up if you don't know what that means). The fact of the matter is the aquarium could hold only so much. The professor wanted to get the most out of the space while including all of the materials that he wanted to store in the aquarium. Why did he put the baseballs in first? Why not the water? To truly maximize the space available, he had to start with the largest object and go in descending order. This allowed every nook and cranny to be filled by the subsequent smaller somethings (again with the alliteration). He wasted no space at all. If he had added the items in any other order, he would have lost space. So what was his first step? Well, first he had to *prioritize*. If he had gone in blindly and dumped the BBs and then the water, he would have had a few floating baseballs instead of being able to dump in the entire bag.

You may think that you're too busy to do that extra reading, but you're not. More accurately, you could say that you have placed doing the extra reading at the bottom of your priority list and you will never get to it. Don't lie to yourself. You may think your aquarium is full, but it could probably just be filled up in a smarter manner. Remember how busy you thought you were in high school, but you realize now that you weren't all that booked? If only someone had told you that you would be much busier in college. What if someone told you that college life gives you more free time than the "real world" would ever allow? Would you believe that? Same story, different page.

So there, now you can't really say that you are too busy. What was the other excuse? Oh yeah, if the professor isn't going to grade the reading assignment, then why should you do it? This is a very common mindset among students. In fact, this is likely the prevailing, default opinion of most college students. It would seem then that it is time for the *talk*. No, not *that* talk. *That* is probably contributing to your daydreaming in class, texting when you should be studying, Facebook-stalking instead of reading, partying too much and too late, and overall lack of sleep (to name a few) in the first place. No, it is time for the "why are you actually here" talk. It's much less graphic and you probably know less about this one going in to it.

For the typical college student, most of your educational experiences have gone something like this: Sit in a class you care nothing about, listen to a teacher who is not particularly engaging, take notes from a screen, study said notes the night before the quiz/test, take the test, get a decent grade, repeat. Sound familiar? Well let's keep going. What if you were asked to tell me the capital of New Hampshire? Uh-oh. What if you had to list the causes of World War II or give the periodic number for the element copper? Crap. Did you answer Concord for the capital of New Hampshire? No? Did you when you were in fourth grade? Probably. It is doubtful that you did very well on the other questions either. Why is this? Most likely it is because of the most dubious distinction in all of education. It is the difference between *memorizing* and *learning.* This distinction is the basis for the *talk.* Why would you need to know the capital of New Hampshire? Barring a guest appearance on *Are you Smarter than a 5th Grader?,* you wouldn't. You can look it up in five seconds from your smart phone. That's why it's called a smart phone; it seems to know everything. But you, however, do not. Because you *memorized* it during your prepubescence. You slept since then. You forgot, mainly because you didn't care in the first place. Forgetting your state capitals or how to make a correct uppercase cursive letter "Z" will probably never come back to bite you. However, if you plan to just memorize your way through college, you are opening yourself up to a whole new possibility of trouble. You see, for many professions, a college education is necessary because the employer sees that you *already* know what they need you to know. If you got hired to fill in the state capitals on a map, many of you would get fired on the first day. You have to *learn* the material.

So, back to the question of why you are enrolled in college. Let's call a spade a spade. You are most likely here to get a "good education" so you can get a "good job" and live a "good life." This is more efficiently described as you want to make a lot of money. Fair enough? No problem. You are in the same boat as most college students. However, to be really successful, both while in college and afterward, you must transition from *memorizing* to *learning.* There will be much more in this book regarding this concept, but one way to get in this mindset is to realize that, although many may disagree with you, your professors aren't the source of all knowledge. Even if they only "test" over what they say in class or include on a PowerPoint slide, there is much more to know. Learning the material is completely dependent on *you*. Think about it this way: Fast forward your life until you are 35 years old and you have a professional career. Say you need to know the answer to a very important question in your field. How are you going to gather the necessary information? Are you going to call your college professor and say, "I've got my pen and paper ready, please proceed with a lecture on the topic of _____?" No. That is not the way adults learn new things. They read to find information. The 35-year-old you would *read*. So why then, when you are paying a fortune to be enrolled in college courses and you've set aside this time in your life to receive the necessary education to be successful for the rest of your life, would you only rely on learning what the professor tells you during class? That is not practice for the real world. That is one of the most sterile, artificial learning environments possible. You will never learn that way again. You should take this current opportunity to dedicate your actions to meaningful experiences that actually mimic what you will be required to do for the rest of your life. You simply cannot get better at learning from print if you never subject yourself to learning from print. Obvious, huh?

So, the reasons for doing that additional reading are very well founded and legitimate—we've established that. We've also effectively debunked your excuse about not having any time. Now it's just awkward. If you want to really get motivated to do all of the work (whether it is extra work or not) to be successful in college and in life, just do this short exercise. Write down (in full sentences) the exact reason(s) that you are choosing to not put forth the effort to do the work. Remember, it shouldn't have anything to do with time—you can slay that beast. If you are truthful, your sentences will be an indictment of your work ethic. It might say something like this:

> *I am choosing not to read the chapter my professor assigned because I am tired. I woke up at 9:30 A.M., went to two whole classes and then got back to my apartment at 2:00 P.M. I would rather watch reruns of "The Fresh Prince of Bel-Air" for a couple of hours and then make a Hot Pocket. My friends are coming over tonight to play Call of Duty and then watch "Monday Night Football," so I'd better get a nap before they get here.*

Yikes. That doesn't exactly sound like the guy a company would want to hire or a woman would want to marry. Sounds a whole lot more like a guy who would be content living in his parents' basement, eating Doritos straight out of the bag.

You are in college for a very small percentage of your life. If you are here for four years and you live to the ripe old age of 85, then you were in college for less than 5 percent of your life. However, how you spend that 5 percent will affect how you live your remaining years. There aren't very many jobs that pay people to sit around watching '90s television reruns and play video games. You might want to use your time for something a bit more productive.

> • **CCSS.ELA-Literacy.CCRA.R.1** Read closely to determine what the text says explicitly and to make logical inferences from it; cite specific textual evidence when writing or speaking to support conclusions drawn from the text.

How do I set up a study situation where I can actually get some work done?

It is not an uncommon occurrence to have every good intention of engaging your mind in an intense study session only to realize that after about ninety minutes, you've accomplished nothing. Why does this always seem to happen? You're trying to get ahead by using that free time for studying, but something always gets in the way. There are a few things that you are probably doing wrong, but they should be easily fixed. Let's take a look at the *who, what, where, when,* and *why* of study sessions.

Who: Who are you studying? If it's your study partner, well, that's not beneficial and can certainly be distracting. That type of "studying" in pairs is not what we're talking about here. The "who" is *you* (for fear of sounding too much like Dr. Seuss, that will be the end of this sentence). You will likely not study in pairs or groups very often. If you do, those sessions are generally to allow for conversations to explain or clarify points of confusion. Those types of study experiences are more like *learning* sessions than *study* sessions. Most of the time you will be studying alone. This is a good thing, because you are the boss and you can control the situation.

What: It doesn't really matter *what* you are studying. If, for any reason, you feel that the material is important to know, then you will likely have to study. There are more specific tips on how to remember/learn information elsewhere in this book.

Where: This is an important one—where you study matters greatly. If you have been experiencing problems with getting anything done while you study, you should first take a look at where you are studying. A very common place for students to want to study is in their room of the dorm or apartment. This isn't always a bad thing, but there are some things to consider. If you live in a dorm, your room is likely shared with a roommate and there is probably a lack of furniture (and hygiene, for that matter). This could be problematic for two reasons: One, your roommate is probably a babbling fool who never shuts up and chews with his mouth open. It's hard to focus on your studies when your stall mate is slurping mac and cheese like it was the last day before his diet (like he always claims it is). That other person in the room is distracting. Number two is the lack of a place to study. Seeing this predicament, you likely settle on the bottom bunk. Luckily, your roommate is feasting in a chair at his desk and you have no real fear of the top bunk finally giving way to his girth, effectively ending your life. So, what do you do? You cozy up on the bed. Bad move. Asking your brain to commit its energies to focusing intently on inherently boring material so you can become familiar with it, remember it, and truly learn it, is a different signal than snuggling up with grandma's homemade afghan. Your brain can't handle those conflicting signals. Since studying is hard work and getting drowsy in the warmth of the bed is quite natural and easy, guess which one wins out? Well, how many times have you woken up with a textbook on your chest?

The point is that you should study in a place that is quiet and not altogether very comfortable. That also means that you shouldn't rest your pretty little head on your balled up fist, also known as God's pillow. You should tell your brain in every way that you are about to engage in hard work, that it is purposeful, and that you are in it for the long haul.

When: This is not a dichotomous question, as many students seem to think. This is not a "do I study or do I not study?" question. The question is *when*, not *if*. First of all, you should study often. Waiting for three weeks until the night before the test to tackle 135 pages of text and 32 pages of notes is not a good plan. You should study in smaller chunks throughout those three weeks. But when? Well, you should never study when you're really tired. It's common for college students to "pull an all-nighter" because they've done no studying before a big exam. The research on this is clear: Do not pull an all-nighter! You need to sleep for your brain to adequately process the information it has learned. In fact, if you do not sleep, you make it difficult to comprehend what you're reading and even more difficult to remember what you've already studied. It's actually counterproductive. Study until 2 A.M. or so and then get a few hours of sleep. Get back at it at 6 A.M. and then promise that you'll never put yourself in that position again.

You should also study as soon after a class meeting as possible. There are many things that will be presented while you are in class that you will have a hard time understanding, or even remembering, weeks later. Your notes will make more sense (and you will be able to add to them) when you review them soon after you initially wrote them down. If you do this after every class meeting, the big study session before the exam will be much more manageable.

Why: Because you want to do well on the test and in the class. You want to know it—not just memorize it. Because you want to get a good GPA that semester, as well as for your entire career. Because you want to graduate with a degree that allows you to get a good job so you can provide for a family. Because you want options in your life and do not want to be nailed down to a dead-end career/ life. Because you want to do fun things and buy nice things. Because you want all of these things for your kids, too, when they are born. That's probably enough reasons why. Or you could play Xbox instead because studying is "stupid" and that class is too hard. Oh, and because your professor is an idiot. Yeah, just play Xbox.

Multitasking

Do you feel that you do not have time to complete everything? You are so overloaded with work that multitasking is the only way anything gets finished, right? Do you listen to music while reading? Do you watch the ballgame or paint your toes while studying? These are common behaviors for students because we often give our brains too much credit. The truth is your brain cannot devote the necessary attention to each task when "multitasking." In reality you are "half-tasking" each activity, resulting in a poor quiz grade and sloppy toenails. To demonstrate, let's think of a few scenarios that we've all experienced. Have you ever been in a busy shopping mall dutifully hunting for the best holiday bargains when you notice that your favorite song is playing over the sound system? Chances are, you didn't notice any songs being played prior to your favorite tune, nor will you attend to the selections being played afterward. Why did you hear only the one song? The answer is: you didn't. Your brain processed all of the music (and other noise) collected by your ears. Most of the information was deemed unnecessary by your subconscious and therefore ignored. However, when your favorite song was processed, you immediately recognized it as being familiar and attended until it was finished. It is much the same as when you are in a crowd of people, all of whom are talking, and you quickly turn your head in the appropriate direction when someone says your name. Maybe he was talking to you, maybe he wasn't,

---

Sleep

We all love it and most of us would claim that we need more opportunities to sleep. Why is it that we often forfeit sleep at the most inopportune times? Have you ever procrastinated for so long that you've been forced to pull an "all-nighter"? If you're like most people, you crashed pretty hard afterward. Although foregoing sleep to get the job done is seemingly necessary, it may not be the most efficient course of action. Your brain needs sleep to concentrate. One of the first side effects of sleep deprivation is the ability to maintain focused attention and as soon as that train starts rolling, it's hard to stop. If you aren't paying proper attention to what you are reading, you will not comprehend nor will you remember. Does your mind ever wander while you are reading a boring assignment? When you get to the end of the page, do you often think "what did I just read"? Chances are, you weren't paying enough attention to comprehend and remember. Have you ever been talking on the phone and decided to clean up the house a bit, only to realize the next day that you cannot remember where you put your car keys? These things happen when we don't pay attention to what we're doing—either because another task is requiring our focus or because we are too tired to devote the mental energy to the task.

If you get too tired to attend well, there is a good chance that anything you do after that point is futile. Sometimes this can give us false hope. You may think that you are ready for that Chemistry final because you spent so much time "studying" the night before. Unfortunately, you may be sadly mistaken come test time if you did not pay attention to what you were doing due to lack of sleep.

Finally, if your academic success isn't a good enough reason to get a restful night's sleep, consider this: lack of sleep also causes weight gain. Without getting too technical, a lack of sleep causes an increase in stress hormones and an imbalance in the two hormones that control your appetite (you can probably guess what happens as a result). So, prioritizing sleep may pay off in the classroom and on the scale.

---

but you noticed nonetheless. Again, your brain is processing all of the information to determine what is important and what needs to be ignored.

It is important to say that if you are in an environment in which nothing will stand out as being important or recognizable, you can likely focus on the task at hand. This would be the difference in reading your textbook at a train station as opposed to in your dorm room where three of your friends are talking about "Dancing with the Stars." Or the difference between listening to Beethoven instead of Lady Gaga on your iPod while studying for your American History exam.

So, next time you are deciding when and where to study, choose an environment that allows you to fully focus on the task at hand, unless of course your test will include questions about reality television and subpar popular musicians.

Have you ever noticed that traffic signs have been edited down to just the essential word(s)? Take the word stop, for instance. There may be ten very good reasons that you should stop your car at a particular place that you see this sign but they are not listed there for you. Instead, the connoisseurs of signs and deciders of where they go whittled down all those reasons to just one word, stop. It really tells you all you need to know. You should cause your car, truck, motorcycle, horse, or travel-mode-of-your-choice to come to a complete halt. They do the same thing with yield and other one-word traffic commands. There is something to be said for that directness and brevity. Immediately, when you see those signs, you know what is expected of you and why. Boiling down your notes to just a couple of essential "signs" can do the same thing for you as you make notes that aid your learning and your preparations for exams.

- **CCSS.ELA-Literacy.CCRA.R.1** Read closely to determine what the text says explicitly and to make logical inferences from it; cite specific textual evidence when writing or speaking to support conclusions drawn from the text.

Part II

Check Yourself before You Wreck Yourself

Chapter

6. I feel like I missed some basics in reading. What does every student, parent, and adult need to know about reading?

7. How can I know what the important parts are of what I am reading?

8. How do I put the "active" in active reading?

9. What does setting "a purpose for reading" have to do with comprehension?

10. How can I read so that I can remember what I read?

11. How can something I read mean more than it says?

12. How can I possibly know what the author is thinking or what he wants me to know?

Chapter 6

I feel like I missed some basics in reading. What does every student, parent, and adult need to know about reading?

Remember when you thought the A, B, C's were fun? You did at one time. You loved the letters in your name. I once heard of a kid that cried when she realized that other people could use the same letters as were in her name—she thought those letters were hers alone. You might not have been quite that attached, but when you first got a glimmer that those squiggles were very important to adults they became important to you, too. You were slowly (or not) moved toward understanding that each letter made a "sound." Which in itself is not true. The letter "c" has no sound of its own—it either sounds like "s" or "k." There is no "c" sound. It gets even more complex. There are 44 (or so, depending on whose interpretation you follow) sounds for the 26 letters of the alphabet. It didn't take long before you became very suspect of this whole letter/sound/phonics thing. In some classrooms, phonics is a tool. In other classrooms, you "do" phonics well or there is something wrong with you. It might surprise you to know that there are millions of people (millions and millions) who learned to read without this so-called essential, one-true-path to reading. Back before the one-true-path method (phonics-or-death approach) you learned how the English language "generally" works (and that is the best promise phonics can make) by . . . (wait for it) . . . reading. You likely started by reading alphabet books over and over again in the lap of some fantastic relative or adult who had the patience to say the words and then let you say the words. Pretty soon you knew all the words on the page. Your parents might have pooh-poohed this by saying, "Oh, she just has it memorized." And they were right. You did have it memorized and you still do. But you were also internalizing how letters fit together to form words, how to know a new word based on words you had already learned, and you got to have the most precious prize of all: A love for the letters, words, sounds, and stories or information that is the beauty of reading.

While phonics is a great tool for readers to use to unlock new words, it is highly cognitive. In other words, it takes a great deal of thinking, processing, and holding information in short term memory while your brain runs through all the rules, exceptions, and generalizations to try and categorize the letters or combinations of letters. If people never moved past the step-by-step processes of phonics to a level of *automaticity* (performing the task without realized effort or forethought), reading would be extremely exhaustive and cripplingly slow. Fortunately, we do reach the level of automaticity and the more we read, the more that is finessed and enhanced. In fact, we never achieve a level with literacy where we have reached a pinnacle; we get better our whole lives.

Another great boost to learning to read is the development of a large repertoire of *sight words*—words that we recognize instantly. The importance of sight words is underscored by the number of irregularly spelled words in the English language that defy sound/symbol analysis. Words like *which, once, would, thought,* and *laugh* are examples of sight words. By the time we become adults our sight word vocabularies are in the thousands and thousands. Building a sight word vocabulary takes repeated readings, many varied reading experiences, and a proclivity to word play. The larger your sight word vocabulary, the more fluently you can read. The more fluently you can read, the less your comprehension is disrupted by having to dual-process and attend to decoding. Win, win.

While there are both skills and strategies involved in the processes of reading, you should know that reading is not something that we do innately. Language (speaking/communicating) is innate—it is also sophisticated and uniquely human. However, decoding squiggles and assigning meaning to them is not centered in any part of your brain. Instead, several parts of your brain have to be "drafted" to leave their primary duties (usually involved in keeping you alive) so that they can all gather together for this act called reading. If any essential part of your brain decides to go back to its original job, well, you just stopped reading. Perhaps you have experienced this phenomenon: You are reading and comprehending, then your brain signals you that you are hungry. You keep reading but now you are also running a list of all the snack food in the house and soon you realize that, while you have been "calling words" quite accurately, you no longer know what you just read. A part of your brain (let's call him Clyde) left to go do his other job and without all the necessary parts of your brain playing along and helping out, no comprehension occurred. This unbelievably complex system of bringing together sensory receptors, perceptual functions, the activation of schema (everything you have ever experienced or know), and combining those processes with the thinking needed to construct understanding makes reading nothing less than a miracle. Yet children as young as four or five learn to read and it is an absolute expectation that every six-year-old in the United States read by the end of first grade. For most children reading happens without struggles, however if anything interferes (for example, sickness, losing a parent, divorce, attending a variety of schools, developmental delays) with the learning that needs to take place during Kindergarten and first grade, then kids will struggle. Reading is necessary for all other learning. A delay in learning to read puts kids in line for dropping out of high school and many other educational hardships.

So, what are the basics you might have missed that would boost your understanding of the reading process? Let's start with comprehension. There is no purpose for decoding except for understanding what is read. In fact, there are many that argue that without comprehension, real reading did not happen. There is also no such thing as reading without thinking. Many people assume that the meaning is in the print of whatever you are reading. It is true that some of the meaning is in the words on the page. But there are very few if any times when *all* the meaning is in the words. Writers expect us to bring something to the table when we read. It is not possible for them to tell us everything about any particular topic. They expect that readers will make inferences, connect to previous knowledge, and construct meaning from the words they put on paper. All of those processes involve thinking.

If you could change two things from the current way you approach print it should be to very deliberately be *active* in your reading, and to change your *attitude* toward reading. Generate your own mental questions about what you want to learn. Pause and reflect on what you are learning as you read. Stop and reread when you find that something doesn't make sense. Look for clues the authors give you to help you more clearly understand what they want you to know. Reading is not passive.

Your attitude toward pretty much everything in your life dictates how good you are at things. We do things we like to do. If you have found yourself saying, "I hate to read." Then you are not likely to get any better at it. We avoid things we hate. There are some very good reasons why you may not like to read at this stage in your life. There has been way too much emphasis on skills, tests, worksheets, tests, drills, and tests. You got to do everything with reading . . . except read. Yes, people do read for pleasure, recreation, and enjoyment, but they are enjoying the mental process as much as the story. Letting a book take you into another time or dimension is not the same thing as zoning out. It is just the opposite. It is zoning in. And it feels really, really good.

It is much more likely that you spent a large quantity of time on decoding skills than on comprehension skills. Just in case you missed or forgot some of the basics, we will include a quick overview for you.

Decoding

Vowels:

Always: a, e, i, o, u

- they can say their names (long sound);

- they can make their short sound;

- they can all make the schwa sound (soft "uh" found in unaccented syllables)

Sometimes: y and w are vowels

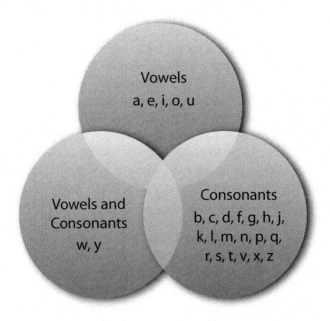

Vowel Combinations:

Diphthongs: oi, oy, ou, ow (boil, boy, bound, cow)
NOTE: ou and ow are not always diphthongs—they are only diphthongs when they make your mouth open widely (just say "cow" and look in the mirror—you'll get it).

Vowel Digraphs: Any combination of vowels that do not make the sound of either of the vowels.
NOTE the "au" in taught. Did you hear an "a" (long, short or the "uh" of a schwa)? No, you did not. Did you hear a "u" (long, short or the "uh" of a schwa)? No, you did not. The "au" makes the same sound as the "aw" in saw, which is also a vowel diagraph as neither the "a" nor the "w" (which is a vowel because it is at the end of a word) is sounded. Another vowel digraph is the double "o" in the word *food* and *look.* In other words, they had to invent a name for what happens when two renegade vowels partner up and decide not to go by any rules whatsoever. Vowel digraphs are only a "thing" because they are not any of the other things. Now does it make sense to you that these things never made sense to you?

Consonants:

All the other letters of the alphabet except the vowels (a, e, i, o, and u and sometimes y and w) are consonants. They are not nearly as tricky as vowels and we can trust them more to be more constant in what they do. Here's the heads up on two quirks that make a difference with consonants.

Consonant Blends:

When consonants (in the same syllable) are adjacent to each other they can form a consonant blend (the letters slide together when voiced but you can still slightly hear each of the two letters, for example, bl, cl, fr, str).

Consonant Digraphs:

A consonant digraph occurs when two adjacent letters make only *one* sound (sh, ph, ch, th, ng, gh, ch) that is not related to the individual sound of either letter. Why does this matter? Because with words you do not know this gives you an instant "rule" that will work for you. You can trust that the digraphs listed above are going to make one sound regardless of where they fall in a word.

The best way to pronounce a big (multisyllabic) word is to break it into syllables. You were taught to do this, but you may not have realized why it mattered how many syllables were in a word or why in the world you would want to break a word into parts. Here is the thing you were either never told, or you were told and didn't care enough to remember:

All the following phonics generalizations apply to the syllables within the big words:

1. Every syllable must have a vowel.
2. When a syllable ends in a consonant and has one vowel, the vowel has a short sound, for example, bit, bat, bet, cot, duck, fish.
3. When two vowels are together in a word, the first one usually makes a long sound and the second is silent (for example, boat, meet, say). NOTE: Vowel combinations of oi, oy, ow, ou (diphthongs) do not follow this rule.
4. When a syllable ends in a silent "e," the vowel that comes before the silent "e" is long (for example, lake, cave, kite, hope, use).
5. When a syllable ends in a vowel and is the only vowel, that vowel is usually long, (for example, later, me, open, unicorn, by).

To tackle an unknown multisyllabic word, first break the word into syllables. Try this word:

accoutrements

1. You know each syllable has to have a vowel.
2. You know that double letters are usually divided.
3. Try saying the word—every time your chin drops down it indicates a new syllable. My chin dropped four times.

ac·cou·tre·ments

4. Since the syllable /ac/ has one vowel and ends in a consonant, I know the /a/ is short.
5. Since the /ou/ does not make my mouth open wide, I know it is not a diphthong (as in count), therefore it makes the same sound as /oo/ (as in spoon).

6. At this point you should be able to pronounce accouterments correctly. The word means "accessories," by the way.

Try this one (*Hint:* there are 5 syllables):

sesquipedalian

Look it up online at dictionary.com and check to see if you marked the syllables correctly. Then take a stab at pronouncing it. Check your pronunciation online and then read the definition. Fitting, huh?

That is as hard and as easy as it is to tackle big words, regardless of where you run across them. At first, this is slow, but it beats the daylights out of guessing at or skipping (don't even go there) words you do not know. The chances of misunderstanding what you are reading if you do that are, well, Brobdingnagian.

So, let me guess. You scanned through all that information about word identification because you have it down pat, right? After all, every six-year-old in America must demonstrate that they understand all that. Just for giggles, try your hand at demonstrating your proficiency.

_____ 1. The second syllable of the nonsense word **blofishtic** would be expected to rhyme with
   a. nise.
   b. dish.
   c. kith.
   d. stick.

_____ 2. The second syllable of the nonsense word **melash** would most likely rhyme with
   a. sea.
   b. hot.
   c. trash.
   d. low.

_____ 3. The second syllable of the nonsense word **alithpic** would be expected to rhyme with
   a. aright.
   b. brick.
   c. kith.
   d. pyth (as in python).

_____ 4. The first syllable of the nonsense word **botem** would most likely rhyme with
   a. coat.
   b. hot.
   c. rah.
   d. low.

_____ 5. Which of the four words below contains a consonant blend?
   a. chop
   b. ship
   c. that
   d. sleep

_____ 6. A diphthong is best illustrated by the vowels representing the sound of
   a. ow in snow.
   b. ou in mouse.
   c. oo in foot.
   d. ai in said.

Write the silent letters on the line beside the words:

_____ 7. climb

_____ 8. rhyme

_____ 9. Doubt

_____ 10. knob

_____ 11. oh

_____ 12. mallard

_____ 13. honest

_____ 14. gnaw

_____ 15. knoll

_____ 16. hour

_____ 17. limb

_____ 18. thigh

_____ 19. calf

_____ 20. moisten

Identify the **BOLD** section of each of the following words:

_____ 21. **dr**op

a. a consonant blend

_____ 22. n**oi**se

b. a consonant digraph

c. a diphthong

_____ 23. r**ai**l

d. a vowel digraph

_____ 24. **ch**in

_____ 25. **cl**am

_____ 26. si**ck**

_____ 27. lo**u**d

_____ 28. **gn**at

_____ 29. fr**ei**ght

_____ 30. The sound of the *schwa* is represented by
a. the a in baited.
b. the e in early.
c. the e in happen.
d. the w in show.

_____ 31. The word **if** ends with the same sound as
a. the ph in graph.
b. the f in of.
c. the gh in taught.
d. the gh in ghetto.

_____ 32. How many syllables are in the word "🐘"?
a. 3
b. 2
c. 4
d. mammals don't have syllables

Image © Sarawut Padungkwan, 2013. Used under license from Shutterstock, Inc.

(See answers on page 158)

Regardless of how well or how poorly you did on those isolated skills, remember that the ultimate goal is comprehension. Word recognition skills, especially phonics, are just tools. Being able to define a *vowel diagraph* is not the point. The point is that when you see one you know immediately what type of behaviors those sounds will *most likely* have. The proper names of the functions of our sound system (phonics) are useless without knowing how those understandings help you unlock unknown words and generally understand how to make sense of the English language. You need to look at those unknown words to discern syllables and know that the syllables *may* conform to the generalizations of our sound system.

Reading is just that simple, and just that complex. And, guess what, we all do it the same and differently at the same time. We are the same in that we are taking symbols (letters) and associating them with sounds, which make words. Then the words are used in conjunction so that the meanings of the individual words are woven together to allow us to understand complex concepts. We are all different in that the way my brain processes each step of that is not exactly the way your brain may work those processes. We may both get the same results while processing quite differently. Now, let's say someone doesn't get the desired result (comprehension). Imagine how hard it is for someone to figure out where his/her processes go offtrack. Or for someone else to figure that out based on behaviors, measurements, or observations.

Any gaps in the way you learned to read are best addressed in the following ways:

1. Read more.
2. Read a variety of different types of print (novels, information books, magazines,editorials, webpages, journals, newspapers, textbooks, etc.).
3. Be metacognitive (think about your own thinking, note how you learn best, attend to what works with your own brain).
4. Engage daily in some form of word play (crossword puzzles, anagrams, Words with Friends, any one of the thousands of online and hand-held games).

How can I know what the important parts are of what I am reading?

For most of us, if we are reading something that we did not choose on our own to read, we either see everything as important, or worse, nothing as important. It is a matter of mental discipline to learn how to discern what the author intends as the important parts of a text.

The first thing you need to do is alert your brain as to what is coming its way. Think of your brain as a huge filing cabinet that is filled with folders. Each folder contains information based on your experiential background—some of these are spawned from actual experiences and others from things you have read, heard, or understood from the world around you (including all types of media). To take in new information, your brain needs to find some way of connecting it to information that is already there. When you send an alert to your brain that new information is coming, you need to get it to open the most likely folder you have related to that topic. If you *do not know* what the topic is, you cannot send that signal. Sometimes the title of a chapter or article is so descriptive that your brain automatically jumps to the folder you need. Most of the time it is not that simple. You have to do a bit more prep than that.

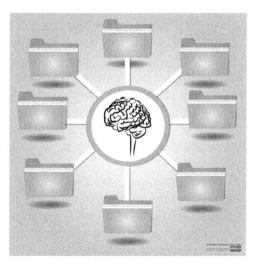

Image © mamanamsai, 2013. Used under license from Shutterstock, Inc.

It turns out that what you enjoyed at five is still a good starter: pictures/illustrations. Immediately, signals are sent to your brain that start to weed out all the superfluous topics and hone in a bit closer on the real target. No pictures? Bummer! Then focus your attention on the structures of the text: titles, heading, subsections, sections, and callout boxes. An abstract or introduction tells you what you are about to read. And, conversely a summary at the end of a piece tells you what you just read. Your goal should be to know what the big idea of a piece is in a matter of about 60 seconds or less.

Attack the Print

Image © schab, 2013. Used under license from Shutterstock, Inc.

Fly into the chapter, article, whatever-type-of-print like you are on fire. Work like the entire book will disintegrate in a matter of 60 seconds. If you go in sloppy and unfocused, you still won't know what is going on in 60 minutes, much less 60 seconds. Be alert and aggressive. Grab one piece of paper and one writing implement. Give yourself exactly one minute to record all you possibly can. Do not take the time now to write in complete sentences. This is quick and dirty. Once you get the hang of this, you will see what works best for you—words, drawing something, inventing your own graphic organizer. The point is that you cannot skip this step. If you do, then you are on your own and your brain will be fighting you every step of the way. This is the primary reason so many people self-diagnose as having attention deficit disorder. You absolutely do have an attention problem when you try to process information without engaging your brain and specifically asking it to attend.

Sometimes you will hear about the brain alert phase called "**surveying** the text." What we are suggesting you do is *surveying on steroids.* You need a good, firm, specific signal sent to your brain to get it ready to retrieve what you already know about the topic you have discovered and to get ready to receive more information. Now that your brain is engaged, you are cooking with peanut oil! The words/terms/headings you wrote on your notes page mean that you have announced to yourself (your brain) what the focus/topic of the reading will be. You might even want to say the topic out loud as you read from your notes page. Whether you put the main topic in the center of the notes page and drew a circle around it or simply made a list on the page of the title, headings, and other info that jumped out at you from the page, you now have a direction by which you can formulate a purpose.

Without a purpose for reading, your brain is quickly going to abandon you in hope of more important tasks—like monitoring your breathing, keeping your heart pumping, making mental notes to ask that cute person a few rows up for his/her phone number—that whole "keeping you alive" thing it does. With a purpose duly noted, your brain will stay involved and try to do what it is instructed to do. The most effective way to keep your brain connected to the task is to get it to look for something. Take the words/terms/headings you jotted down on your notes page and ask **questions**. "What is a _____," "What does it have to do with _____," "What are the processes/purposes of _____," are examples of the types of questions you might quickly jot down. If you are asking questions, you will likely find answers. If your questions are targeting the main words/terms/headings, then your answers should be a fleshing-out of the ideas/information therein. You have now whittled down the forest (a whole wordy chapter) to the most essential trees (important parts).

Now, and only now, you are ready to **read**. You are looking in earnest now for the important parts. Most textbooks give you clues, hints, and do everything but add flashing lights to help readers find the main points the authors want to get across. They include these aids, but it is up to you to use them. I have played the "get to the point" game myself—flipping through the text to the exact page for the assigned chapter, deliberately ignoring everything except the paragraphs and reading as fast as possible just to say I read it. What a waste of time! You need a plan of attack to get the most out of the least time.

This is a list of the most useful text features for information books (textbooks fit in this category). The list indicates the name of the part of the book and why you might ever want to look there:

Text Features

Parts of a Book	What It Really Is	Why in the world I would use this?
Table of Contents	The Part You Should Always Read	Boring list of yada-yada . . . or secret to knowing how to alert your brain? All the work is done for you. Some Tables of Contents include not only the title of the chapter, but also all subheadings and even summaries in only a couple of sentences. If you luck into books that do all that then much of the surveying/previewing of the chapter is done for you. Stick a fork in that!
Index	The Absolute Shortcut to Finding What You Are Looking For	Now get this—they took all the important words, terms, and concepts in the book and put them in a big alphabetized list in the back of the book. It screams "look here, look here!"
Glossary	Prelocated and Defined Terms	They anticipated the words you would FOR SURE need to know and put them in alphabetical order with the definitions that match the way the words/terms are used in the book. This is not the "look up the words in the back of the book and write the definition" time-sucker of middle school. This is the "you have got to be kidding me" easy-peasy way to know what new terminology means.
Appendix	One Less Google Search	In case you are unsure of the meaning of some concept, they added additional information in this section (could be at the end of each chapter—could be at the end of the book). Need to do research on a topic in the book? They may have already done the footwork on that and included it in the appendix. This is not at all like the appendix in your body—you can actually live without that one!

Features within the Reading	Flashing Lights of a Blue Light Special	Why in the world I would use this?
Bold, *Italicized*, or colored Words	**Please** *read* **me!!**	After the authors finished writing they went back and put emphasis on the *important* parts so they would be **easy for you to find**. In other words, they are pointing the finger at *Waldo* and shining a spotlight on him.
Bulleted Lists	Premade, Perfect Notes Courtesy of the Author. You Are Welcome!	• To the point • Essential • Few words • Begs you to read them
Headings and Subheadings	Hello, Brain? Oh, Hello Brain! Could I Have Your Attention, Please?	Literally tells you what to get your brain to connect to. No hunting, no tricks, no kidding. Pay attention to the subheadings—they show you all the "parts" of the real topic.
Pictures, Diagrams, Graphs, Maps, Charts (and the like)	Anything That Takes Up Space and Is Not a Paragraph	 easy to skip pretty do not skip! shows relationship explains in images much information in few words when you first see when you look closer wooser!
White Space	Borders	Believe it or not you are paying extra for more space with no words. True story. Publishers are making the left, right, top and bottom borders on the pages wider to allow you room to make notes. Make notes!!
Callout Boxes	It Is Like They Read Your Mind!	You were just sitting there wishing they would put a freaking box around the important parts as you have truly important things to do and these paragraphs drone on and on and on. Despair not. Look for the boxes and callouts. If you are old enough to remember pop-up videos on VH1, then you will know how great it is that they do our thinking for us!

So far you have identified the animal you must slay (surveyed the text) and, set purposes for the work you will do (made questions). If you are still in the game, it is now time to read and make notes. At first pass through a text, you may still be guessing a bit at what will ultimately be important. If you are a college student, you are trying to match what you find as important with what your professors think is important. You will get better at that as the semester goes along. Some professors are better than others (in pretty much every way possible) at guiding you toward what they want you to focus on. If you are provided with guiding questions for assigned readings, reading guides, or other such supportive devices, then you should make good use of those. If the whole assignment is "read chapter 5," then you are on your own. From here on, we separate the men from the boys in terms of making the reading work for you.

After your first read through the material, you will have identified and in some way "marked" your version of the important parts. The next step is to read back through what you selected. Let's say you used a combination of highlighting and note-taking in the margins of the book. Read (skim/scan) through just those parts again. Do they tell anything that sounds like cohesive information? If so, that is a good thing. If it reads like a jigsaw puzzle, then you have likely not been very successful and need to go back and "read around" the parts you marked to see if you can get some more logical thoughts. When you can actually **say** the important parts out loud (and yes, wait till your roommate leaves and **recite** them), then you are ready to close the book. Enjoy your beverage of choice.

Forty-five minutes before you go back to the class for this assigned reading, pull out your book, notebook and make yourself read through (aloud is still good but if you are drawing a crowd you can read silently) your highlights and notes again. This will provide an essential **review** of the information just in time to hear a lecture or participate in class discussions. That's how you find the important parts. With all the aids, strategies, and a little bit of "just do it," locating the important parts will get easier every single time you do it. So much so that soon you will do all this automatically, easily, and expertly.

How do I put the "active" in active reading?

Maybe this has happened to you: You know you need a really **good grade in a certain class or course so you become hyper-vigilant in setting aside time to make sure you get all the assigned reading done.** You even buy a brand new pack of highlighters dedicated just to that textbook. You get everything situated for a nice productive reading of your assignment and start the first paragraph. By the second sentence you have found two sentences that seem very important. By the end of the paragraph, all the sentences seemed important and the page, as well as your fingertips, are beginning to take on a soft yellow glow as you continue to paint the textbook with your highlighter.

When you first started the paragraph you were determined to learn it as you went along. Some sentences you read twice and maybe even read a couple aloud or circled some vocabulary you thought might be important. Now you are the bottom of page 2, you've color-coded until your highlighters are starting to skip, your pages are all but drippy wet, and they look like you smashed a bag of Skittles in your book and baked it at 375 degrees. You experience major mental fatigue and are now unsure that you understand or can recall what you have read so far—and you have determined that every word of every sentence is important.

This scenario amounts to a series of bad reading habits compounded by anxiety, stress, and frustration. Most of us toss the book across the room, see if the ink in a highlighter will ignite with a Zippo, and decide to put our trust in the lecture, our magnificent note-taking skills, and printing all the PowerPoint slides the instructor puts online. Neither book-hurling, smoking highlighters, or worshiping false note-taking/PowerPoint gods will get you where you need to be.

The good news/bad news about discerning key ideas—the important parts—is that:

1. it is a learned set of skills;
2. you can learn to do it well; and
3. it takes work on your part.

Let's get basic. What you need to do with anything you read is:

• **Know what it says**—key ideas/information

• **Know what it means**—understand it and make connections

• **Know how to use what it says**—to learn, to make valid points

Basically, when an author writes something to provide information, they follow a similar path to varying degrees of intricacy:

Step 1: Tell you the thing they want you to know.

Step 2: Tell you other things to help you understand how the main thing works, provide some characteristics of the main thing, and some analogies regarding the main thing that they think will help you understand it more clearly.

Since the author is guessing at how much information to provide to get his audience to understand the main thing, many times he or she includes several sets of all the things in Step 2 listed above. At some point the reader may be so saturated with context and details about the main thing that they no longer remember or recognize the main thing (i.e., Can't see the forest for the trees).

Know What It Says

Reading closely is not about the proximity between your face and a book! Close reading of text requires *action* on your part. When you read actively, you read deliberately. It is not possible to accidentally comprehend. Nor is it possible to automatically comprehend. Close reading of text takes brain energy. It puts a heavy demand on working memory. You have to signal your brain with that little voice in your head and say, "care about this." This signal is linked to the *purpose* for your reading. We do not approach all print the same way. No one strategy works in all reading situations. You must be organized in your approach to reading a piece of print and you have to identify the specifics of how you will tackle the reading to know what it says. You must consider the *author* and understand how who wrote a piece influences how you can know what it says. You also have to get a handle on any vocabulary that is so unknown that you lose the meaning of the passage. Your word knowledge is your key to unlocking meaning. It is something that you work on over a lifetime. Key word there is *work*.

Recap: How do I know what something says?

1. Read actively.
2. Be deliberate in sending signals to your brain.
3. Be organized in strategy use.
4. Read through the lens of the author's perspective.

What are some ways to read actively? One way is tried-and-true: *take notes*. Here is where choice and personal preference plays a big part. Your brain does not care if you write your notes in the margin directly on the book or on a notepad, computer screen, or portable electronic device. That is where you try it different ways and see what works for you. For some people it helps to write in the book, then transfer that information and expand upon it in a notebook, and then to type it into an electronic format that is organized and searchable. The multiple-layers of exposure to the information in that example is part of a process called *overlearning.* Overlearning requires rote memorization by writing or reading the same information over and over again. It works for many people. Doesn't work for many others. It works for some people in certain types of learning and not at all for other types of learning. There is no guide or magic wand to tell you which works for you and when (if at all) it works for you. You have to know how you learn. And that's solely your responsibility. Once you have determined the best way to take notes, then you can make that a staple in your strategy arsenal.

Some people find it helpful to question themselves about a piece before and during reading. Here is what we know: when your interest in a piece of reading goes up, so does your motivation, and therefore your comprehension. You are responsible for getting your brain in the game. By developing questions and then answering those questions you have guaranteed yourself an active reading experience. This is basically an altered method of note-taking that helps you stay focused and interested.

Instant recognition lists is another method that ensures active reading. It is simply a matter of personalizing the print. Each and every time you find an idea, concept, or reference that "rings a bell" with you, you make a notation in the book. Once compiled, these form lists of connections to what you are reading. You can make this stronger and more comprehensive by indicating information that you have questions about (signified by adding a question mark) or other types of shorthand notations.

Many textbooks have valuable information in the form of bars, charts, graphs, and other types of visuals. Our tendency is to skip those. To our eyes, those look like immediate and intense WORK. Our brains would rather not do that, thank you very much. When you are reading complex text on unfamiliar topics and basically you are finding that you are comprehending very little of it, try this: Turn every visual aid into a narrative and every narrative section to a visual aid of your own making. There is no way to convert narrative to image or image to narrative without understanding what you are reading.

Another embellished type of note-taking is to make flash cards. Go through your notes, either from your book or your notebook, and use 3 × 5 cards to record facts, concepts, and any vocabulary you need to learn. This makes quizzing yourself over the content very easy. Reading these and reciting them as you go through the cards provides the repetition needed for overlearning. Overlearning is the ultimate fluency on any subject. Reading or reciting the cards aloud involves more senses and makes it easier to recall the information. In the car for long periods of time? Read the notes into a recorder or your phone and play them back as you drive. Try to anticipate what you are saying next and finish your own sentences/thoughts. These are the types of *rehearsals* that imprint on the brain and further develop neuronal pathways that aid information retrieval.

Know What It Means

At one time in your educational career, knowing the literal meaning of whatever you were reading was just fine. People got excited that you understood it. Not so much anymore. Of course, literal comprehension is a very basic first step, but not a place you need to set up camp and think you are done. Much more will be expected from you now. In information print (nonfiction), you will not only be expected to learn and remember factual information, but also to understand how large concepts fit together, complement each other, overlap with other concepts, and the big picture of "so what," as to the implications of these information pieces on anything that matters. Learning small bits of information in isolation only to feed it back to the instructor on exams is not what college is about. You will be expected to understand the major concepts and all the nuances that are associated with it.

Knowing what you are reading *means* is even more complex in fiction and literary nonfiction (for example, biographies, autobiographies). Every single time you are assigned to read a piece of this type of literature you are asked to know *more than* what it says. What does the author want you to know? What is the author's stance? Why did the author use this word, or that word? What are the implications of (fill in any number of types of queries)? You are left wondering what type of mental telepathy is needed to answer these questions. And the vocabulary! Protagonist, antagonist, denouement, connotation, denotation . . . the list goes on seemingly ad infinitum. The type of reading it takes to conquer literature of this nature is close, repeated, and prayerful. You must read recursively as you make sense of one aspect of the writing and then search back to double-check you are on the right "wave length" with the author, who may have been dead for hundreds of years. You may need to draw timelines, use all types of character analysis charts, graphic organizers, as well as take copious notes throughout. Your saving grace in literary studies is that each time you work through a piece it makes the next one a bit easier. Also, you have to understand that there are people who dedicate their entire professional lives to interpreting the writings of others. Unless you are majoring in English or Literary Studies it is likely that you will have far fewer experiences with literature at the university level and far more emphasis on learning from expository (information) text.

Know How to Use What It Says

You have made sense of what it says. You have wrestled the writing/information to the ground and wrung out what it means (or at least one version of what it means in the case of literature). It's still not time to call it a day. It will be rare at the university level for a professor to let you walk away at that point. You should be daily prepared for any number of "so what" queries. There is value in having a strong foundational knowledge of your discipline (your major). However, there are few jobs for people who just "know stuff." Our world is a problem-generating place and the people who make an impact must be problem-solving people. The "so what" questions are posed to push you to habitually ask:

- So, how does this impact x, y, or z systems?

- So, what actions need to happen at this juncture?

- So, what are the implications of this information?

- Who is impacted?

- In what way are they impacted?

- What does a logic model say needs to happen?

- What does this look like a year out, five years out, 100 years out?

These are the questions that affect societies, medical advancements, the environment, education, cultures, industry . . . the world. This is where true thinking is front and center. Just as you are unique in your appearance, your fingerprints, and your DNA, you are also unique in the way you think. The capacity for you to change the world is within you. For good or for bad, that power is within you. While we all go through some of the same process whereby we solve problems, we each carry a unique ability to look at something in a different way, to act on that thinking in powerful ways. This is the push you will feel—to extend your thinking, prompt you to action, and provide opportunities for you to express yourself.

You do yourself a favor if you anticipate and plan for these opportunities, which may or may not be something you are actually excited about. For one thing, these types of opportunities are extremely labor intensive. You have to use brainpower you don't even realize you have. And, believe it or not, you will actually become better and better at doing this the more times you conquer the questions and related projects that go along with using information/learning that you know and understand.

- **CCSS.ELA-Literacy.CCRA.R.1** Read closely to determine what the text says explicitly and to make logical inferences from it; cite specific textual evidence when writing or speaking to support conclusions drawn from the text.

- **CCSS.ELA-Literacy.CCRA.R.2** Determine central ideas or themes of a text and analyze their development; summarize the key supporting details and ideas.

- **CCSS.ELA-Literacy.CCRA.R.8** Delineate and evaluate the argument and specific claims in a text, including the validity of the reasoning as well as the relevance and sufficiency of the evidence.

What does setting a "purpose for reading" have to do with comprehension?

Remember the *Where's Waldo?* books? Hard to find that little devil, isn't it? Now imagine trying to find him if you had no idea what he looks like. How possible would that be? It is the same with trying to read without a purpose. If you do not know what you are looking for, there is no possible way to see it. One more time: Not looking means not seeing. In fact, if you have not put into words what you are looking for as you read then your brain is not engaged in the pursuit. Here is the sequence:

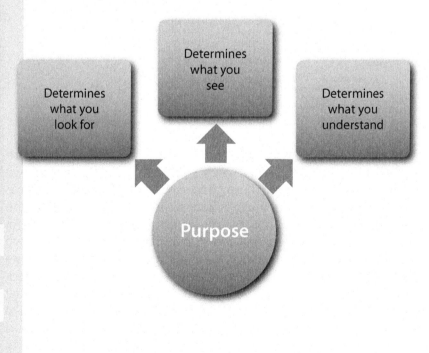

Determines what you see

Determines what you look for

Determines what you understand

Purpose

Without a purpose for what you are reading, you may find your-self simply guessing. Just like looking at every single image in a *Where's Waldo?* illustration and hoping to figure out which one is Waldo with little or no information about what he looks like, it is very exhausting to read something and think that every sentence might be what you are looking for. You are in essence asking your brain to retain this, retain that, make a note here, and remember this-that-or-the-other over and over. Your brain is not designed to take in unrelated data and hold it for you. That pushes your short-term memory to capacity very quickly. It simply is not possible to com-prehend what you are reading without some directive to your brain that indicates why you are reading and what you are looking for.

The progression of reading with a purpose goes something like this:

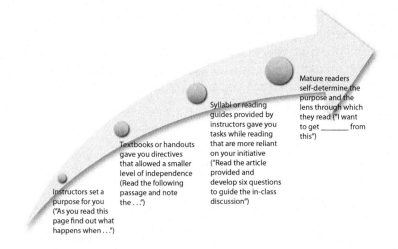

Instructors set a purpose for you ("As you read this page find out what happens when . . .")

Textbooks or handouts gave you directives that allowed a smaller level of independence (Read the following passage and note the . . .")

Syllabi or reading guides provided by instructors gave you tasks while reading that are more reliant on your initiative ("Read the article provided and develop six questions to guide the in-class discussion")

Mature readers self-determine the purpose and the lens through which they read ("I want to get _____ from this")

Mature readers know what they are looking for and therefore can find it much more readily. Once you begin to do this routinely it becomes completely transparent and automatic. You won't even re-alize you are voicing anything in your head. Your brain will get the silent message and your eyes will go about the process to skim, scan, and bring into view the information you need. There are two driving forces that determine the signals you send your brain. One is when someone gives you (mandates) something you must read. With that scenario you may not have an intrinsic need to know what the piece is about or even how to approach it. If the piece is given to you in an instructional setting it might be that you are provided some background information on the topic or at least directed in some way as to what you are attempting to get from the reading. If none of those things are in place and your entire information set related to the reading is "Read Chapter 5," then you will have to do some of the grunt work yourself.

The second scenario is that you have self-selected what you are going to read. It's much easier here. You clearly are interested or have a pressing need to know regarding the piece. It might be an Internet search, an article, or book on a health topic that is personal to you, reviews of new music releases, or some back-and-forth on a hot sports event/topic/scandal. You actually already knew your purpose when you located the print. That is why you find this type of reading so much easier. One, it is interesting to you for some personal reason, and two, you know what you want to find. You have a clear vision. A set purpose for engaging with the print. You leave satisfied every single time. Now, all you have to do is get that momentum going for things that are not necessarily interesting to you and for which you have no intrinsic need-to-know purpose.

This thought process might help you get started:

1. What is this animal?
   b. Quick classification—is it fiction or nonfiction?
   c. Is it a scientific article?
   d. A primary resources like a historical letter/document?
   e. Historical fiction? Mystery? Literary writing?
      Newspaper? Editorial? Essay?

2. What is there to help me?
   a. Are there titles?
   b. Headings?
   c. Subheadings?
   d. Are there charts/graphs/images or callouts?
   e. Is there an abstract or a summary?
   f. If it is electronic, are there related links? Embedded dictionary or thesaurus?

3. Do I already know this author or source (a particular professional journal, perhaps)?

4. Is there any directive to me as to what I am to accomplish with this reading?
   a. Can I restate the directive in my own words?
   b. Is the directive specific enough to give me a targeted purpose?

5. What strategy will I use to mark the text or chronicle what I find?

   a. Text-markup strategy where I code the information as I go along?

   b. Highlighting with margin notes to remind me of what I have found?

   c. Written notes or outline on a piece of paper?

   d. A sketch of how what I am finding is connected, connects with other information, or relates to my purpose?

So, now you read. How do you know if you were successful in understanding what you read? Can you summarize it? If not, then no, you didn't get it. The ultimate test for comprehension is summarization. If you cannot put it into your own words and retell what you read, then not enough thinking has occurred for you to understand it. The smart people stop periodically as they read a long passage and test themselves: Can I retell what I just read? If not, reread, take closer notes, seek another source on the topic that is more within the reading comfort level, and make yourself another (or more) purpose for reading as you start again.

One other aspect you need to consider is the lens you are looking through as you approach any particular reading event. The meaning you get from anything you read is only somewhat embedded in the words you read. You actually construct meaning as you take what you read and determine what it means in terms of what you already know or believe. In other words, the meaning you get from what you read is partially from the actual words that are there, from the context in which they appear, and from your own beliefs, interests, and needs. Real comprehension comes from the tenuous balance of your interpretation of what you read and the context of the reading.

Context confusing you? Try this analogy. Let's say you have just started Stephen King's newest scare-you-to-death book. It is a nice sunny day with a gentle wind so you decide to sit outside. You have a large bottle of water and your only distraction is the sound of the wind in the trees. You consume the premise of whatever type of demon/devil/newly dead creature that King throws at you with a healthy respect, a slight quickening of your heartbeat, but otherwise you are free to become engrossed in the action. You are relaxed and admire King's turn of phrase as you marvel at how many incredibly evil people/things one man can dream up. You close the book deeply satisfied that this story will deliver what you look for in a King novel.

The next time you pick the book up you are housesitting for your grandparents in their 100-year-old house. It is a dark stormy night and outside the thunder, wind, and slanted rain make the panes in the old windows pop and shake in their frames. You settle down on the couch and feel slightly cool so you pull a throw across you. As you start to read, you are overcome with a dread feeling. You try to shake it off, but then the lights flicker, flicker, and go out. Just as you get off the couch the lights pop back on. You tell yourself all is fine and start to read again. It seems to you that King is spending quite a bit of time building up to whatever is about to happen. You are annoyed with the book—just get out of there, you think. You note that your heart is pounding and that you have glanced down the hallway twice. You keep reading white-knuckled as you hear your heart pounding in your ears and still the protagonist (main character in the story who is about to be stabbed, electrocuted, eaten alive, boiled alive, chopped, shredded, etc., you get the idea) goes further in the dark recesses of the forest/house/cave/you-name-it-scary-place. At that point, from absolutely nowhere, your grandmother's cat jumps on your lap and you do everything within your power to gain control of your bladder. Book closed.

Words are the same. Violence and scary level the same. What changed? The context. Other examples of how context changes what you read include:

1. Being asked to read under duress (like when you are arrested).

2. Being asked to read in front of a very important person (think president).

3. Reading when you are worried, sick, embarrassed, anxious, distracted by others, and rushed (list could go on and on).

4. Reading something that is extremely outside your interest level.

5. Reading something that is extremely outside your readability level (too many complex sentences and hard words).

6. Reading something you believe to be a waste of your time.

We tend to oversimplify what it takes to read and comprehend what we read. So many important things have to come together at once and stay together until you have accomplished your reading goals. You may think that if you can just read faster you will have championed all you need. Maybe if you just learned a long list of really hard words you would have all you need to smoothly read anything put in front of you. Could be that you are setting all your hopes and dreams on a couple of really good strategies that you will just plug in and use at your whim. The truth is that without communicating a clear purpose to your brain and considering the lens you look through when you start reading, you will still end up wondering why you don't understand what you read. It is as simple, and complicated, as that.

> • **CCSS.ELA-Literacy.CCRA.R.10** Read and comprehend complex literary and informational texts independently and proficiently.

In many of your courses, you will find your reading assignments either in the syllabus or on the course calendar. The book may not be talked about in class at all, or you may find that the professor stays very close to the chapters in the required books. You may find it quite normal for there to be no support whatsoever given for the reading assignments. No reading guide, purposes set, or assigned activities that go along with the reading to help you focus your attention to the aspects of the chapters the professor wants you to focus on. If you try to read the chapters without any purpose or predetermined strategy (some sort of note-taking), you are taking a huge risk as to this being a good use of your time. In other words, reading passively without set purposes is little better than not opening the book. Don't go there. You will feel underprepared, a bit ripped off, and pretty bitter about taking the time to read the chapter for no payoff.

How can I read so that I can remember what I read?

Let me guess: You read the whole chapter that your professor assigned, but you still failed the quiz? She made the claim that students who failed to read the assignment would have no chance of passing the quiz. You took that scare tactic to heart, marched yourself straight back to your cozy little slice of dorm heaven and didn't get up from the futon until you read every word of that chapter. Why did you fail? You read it! The kid who wears pajamas every morning to class and smells like waffles, he's the one that should have failed the quiz. He doesn't even own the textbook. You, on the other hand, read every word. The injustice is immeasurable. In fact, looking back, it took you almost an hour and a half to read that stupid chapter and you still flunked the quiz. What's the point in reading it at all?

This is an all too common occurrence. Not being able to recall the information after reading a text is certainly frustrating, but there are ways to keep this from happening. Let's rewind the tragic tale of the failed quiz and take a look at what should have happened. You got to your dorm room and breathed a heavy sigh of relief when you noticed that your roommate was gone to class. Perfect—no having to deal with her intrusive questioning or trying to tune out her unhealthy obsession with Nicki Minaj. You plopped down on the futon, kicked off your rain boots, and immersed yourself into the magical world of the 17th century British Parliament. Fast-forward 90 minutes, you self-satisfyingly closed your textbook, put a check mark next to "read history chapter," and set out on the search for a bowl to make your Ramen noodles. Where did you go wrong (besides buying Ramen noodles)? Well, the first thing you should have done was include a few more items when you sat down on the futon— namely a pen and a piece of paper. Every reading experience that you have, particularly when you are reading informational print, should include an *active* component. Does this mean you should put the book under your nose as you're pumping out 50 push-ups? No. It simply means that humans have a very difficult time remembering information that they read *passively.*

Consider this: Have you ever been reading an assignment only to come to the realization that, while your eyes are passing over the words and your brain is calling them out, you are actually thinking about something else? Sure, you're "reading" the fascinating chapter about the British Parliament, but in reality, you're planning what you need to buy at the grocery store. Maybe you actually get finished with the final page in the chapter and think to yourself, "I have no clue what I just read." Just because you *read* it doesn't mean you *comprehend* it. As humans, we have an incredible ability to do multiple things at once. Our brains actually seek to find shortcuts to become more efficient and therefore exert less effort; however, if we do not think about what we're doing, we will have a really hard time remembering anything about it. You may also have experienced this scenario: You're driving somewhere very familiar—let's say you're driving home for fall break. Whether you get caught up listening to the new playlist you put on your iPod or you just get lost in all of the stressful thoughts about the first six weeks of college, you pull into your parent's driveway and think, "Wow, I'm already here?" Your brain took charge of the drive. You obeyed all (OK—*most*) of the traffic laws, you executed all of the turns, effectively avoided killing yourself or another motorist, and *voilà!* You made it home. Yes, you're alive, but you didn't pay a whole lot of attention to what was happening on the way. It's the same thing that happens to us when we read. Yes, we made it to the end of the chapter, but we may not have paid too much attention to what happened along the way. If this happens when we read, we can't remember anything from that darned chapter—and who wants to read about the British Parliament twice?

This scenario happens to all of us. It is very easy to allow our brains to read text passively. It is much more difficult to read the same information actively; however, the difference it makes in terms of true comprehension and eventual recall is drastic. If you want to remember what you read, you must *pay attention.* Stop the presses! This is a novel idea. You can't let your mind wander about spring break escapades or the football game this Saturday. You need every necessary brain process to focus on what you're reading. How can you ensure that your sneaky little brain won't proverbially stab you in the back this way? You give it something to do. You make the reading *active.*

So it makes sense (hopefully) that you must make the reading active to keep your brain from wandering, but how do you make the reading active? Throughout this book you will find strategies that will help keep your brain on track while reading. These aren't the fluffy, roll-your-eyes kind of strategies they teach to people with anger issues like "take a deep breath and count to ten" or "imagine a time in which you weren't angry." The strategies you will have the opportunity to apply are tried-and-true, research-based skills that every good reader needs to have in his or her arsenal. If the ol' "sit down on your bed, open the book to the first page, read every word from left to right until you get to the end of the chapter" strategy is the only arrow in your quiver—you will greatly benefit from practicing these new skills. However, not every strategy will work well for every reader. You will have to try each of them to get a good feel for what works well for you.

The Connection Between Reading and Memory

How well do you remember? If you're like most people, you can remember every word of your favorite song and you'll never forget the toilet-paper-stuck-to-the-shoe incident in middle school. However, when it comes to remembering your mom's birthday or recalling the abbreviations for the periodic table—your memory seems to fail you all too often. Memory is a funny thing. It is often misunderstood and can be your best asset or your worst enemy. Getting your memory to work for you can make all the difference in academic performance, as well as in learning new information effectively. Before we look at ways to better manipulate your memory in your favor, we first must know a little bit more about the types of memory.

Working Memory (Short-Term Memory)—This type of memory requires attention to exist. To illustrate what this means, let's use an example: Suppose that you are with a group of friends and the four of you decide that you are hungry and are craving a pizza. Now let's also suppose that none of you has access to a smartphone to look up the number to your favorite pizza joint (a big assumption, I know—but work with me here). Your solution is to consult the archaic phone book for the number. Once you look up the number, you will repeat the digits in your head (maybe even out loud) until you have dialed each number. If you fail to give repeated attention to each digit, you will likely forget at least one component of the number and that means no pizza—not good. However, because you continuously repeated all of the numbers, you successfully "remembered" how to dial. The reason this type is called "working memory" is because you must use or manipulate the

(continues)

(continued)

information while it is in your conscience. Scientists believe that the average human has the capacity to hold between four and nine unique bits of information in working memory at a time. There are strategies that help with this limitation, but we'll discuss that in a bit.

Long-Term Memory—This is what most people think of when they think about memory. What were the main causes of World War II? Where was I on September 11, 2001? When is my girlfriend's birthday (very important by the way)? Conversion to long-term memory is the goal when we learn new information; however, this process is often very confused. The popular belief is that our memories are stored in a specific part of the brain devoted to that particular information and, when we need to recall the memory, we access that "file" in our brain. Some parts of this belief are true. For example, there is a region of the brain largely devoted to memory called the *hippocampus*. However, most of our memories are not "stored" in a specific location; rather they are neuronal links between bits of information located throughout the brain. These links are established in a specific pattern between neurons, making memory more of a process that a single component. It may help to think of it in this way: Imagine that you are trying to help your best friend remember where he celebrated New Year's Eve a few years ago. Since you were not there, you can only assist by cueing his memory. To do this, you may ask questions like, "What did you wear?" or, "Who did you go with?" You may even ask, "What kind of food did you bring to the party?" Any of these questions could tap in to the memory pattern of that night. Your friend may say, "Oh yeah, I went with John and Michele. They picked me up and I spilled nacho cheese in their back seat. We were on our way to. . . ." Bits of information have been connected to form a cohesive memory.

Gaining a better understanding how long-term memory works helps us when we learn new information and actually want to be able to recall it later. The best way to remember new facts and concepts is to purposefully create links with existing knowledge. When you connect new information with information that already has an established neuronal sequence in your brain, you increase the likelihood of achieving long-term retrieval.

Procedural Memory—If you are an athlete, you are probably familiar with the concept of "muscle memory." It is the reason that golfers can consistently contort their entire body in the exact same way time after time to hit a ball with a club. It is the reason that premiere basketball players can set their feet, bend their knees, and release the ball at the precise moment, with the perfect rotation and arc to make a shot from 20+ feet. It's also why we have the saying, "it's like riding a bike." With repeated practice, our bodies learn to automatically reproduce movements. This is also very important for musicians, as they play the same notes again and again. Procedural memory is attained only through sustained, consecutive practice.

Getting the Most from Your Memory
One of the best ways to address deficits in working memory is to chunk information. You'll recall that a previous section mentions that the average human cannot hold more than nine unique bits of information in working memory at once. However, if you can find a way to collapse those individual bits of info together, you have a fewer number of *unique* pieces to remember, freeing up space in your working memory. Let's look at a classic example of how chunking allows us to better utilize the precious space in our working memory. Take 10 seconds to look at the numbers below:

1 8 1 2 2 0 1 7 7 6 1 4 9 2

Can you remember the order? If you're like most people, you may have recalled about half of the sequence. Now take another 10 seconds to look at these numbers:

1812   20   1776   1492

How'd that go? Again, most people can easily recall all 14 digits in this sequence with no problem. The difference is obvious. Most of the numbers are now chunked into familiar, larger (in this case) years: the War of 1812, the year of our Independence (1776), and the year Columbus allegedly "discovered" America (1492). The only outlier is the number 20, but that isn't too hard to recall. Through chunking, we've essentially turned 14 unique bits of information into four. So, not only can you now remember all 14 digits, but you have more space cleared in your working memory to add more information.

Another quick strategy to help you get the most from your memory is to employ mnemonic devices. This may seem Greek to you at first, but you're likely familiar with some common mnemonic strategies. The usage of rhyming poems, acronyms, and acrostics is quite ordinary in the acquisition and reten- tion of information in grade school. Do you remember what FOIL means when it comes to algebraic binomials? Sure you do; First—Outer—Inner—Last. And you thought you would never see that again. FOIL is an example of using an easily remembered acronym to cue the memory of a more complex order of mathematical operations. Or what about the classic Every Good Boy Does Fine? Why, that's the scaling of a treble clef when reading music (E,G,B,D,F). This acrostic, while similar to an acronym, also serves to help recall a rather arbitrary sequence (E, G, B, D, F) by utilizing a more coherent sentence (Every Good Boy Does Fine). Finally, rhyming can really aid in retention. You already know this

(continues)

(continued)

because you can remember every word to songs that you haven't heard in years. You know the generalized spelling rule "I before E, except after C" because of a rhyme.

Your brain loves to play with language—that's why jokes and puns are often just clever adjustments to words. Most humans have a natural propensity to remember information more efficiently if a mnemonic device is in play. So, next time you're trying to remember the sequence of events leading to the Civil War or the appropriate steps to complete a chemical equation, try creating an acronym or acrostic. You may even turn it into a short rhyme or song that you cannot get out of your head.

I bet you thought the hardest part of a test was taking it, right? Well, maybe not. In this next reading you should develop a test to determine how well others can demonstrate their understanding of what they read. Your test should have 20 questions. You may use any combination of the following:

- Essay
- Multiple-choice
- Matching
- Fill-in-the-blank

The purpose of this experience is twofold: (1) to show you that you will know this passage extremely well before you complete this exercise; and (2) to give you a model for replicating this experience with information you need to "overlearn" in preparation for an upcoming test. Mark the text in this chapter as you read so that you can begin to formulate your questions. Submit both your marked pages and the test you prepare.

- **CCSS.ELA-Literacy.CCRA.R.2** Determine central ideas or themes of a text and analyze their development; summarize the key supporting details and ideas.
- **CCSS.ELA-Literacy.CCRA.R.10** Read and comprehend complex literary and informational texts independently and proficiently.

How can something I read mean more than it says?

Our brains are geared to try and make sense of our world. It is our brain that does its first and most important job—keeping us alive. Everything we hear, see, touch, smell and believe about our surroundings goes through a process of sense-making in our brains. When we read we have to do those same kinds of processes without the direct stimuli that our brain is usually provided. In essence, the word use, the way the text/story comes together, and what we know about the world that is already situated in our schema has to work together to bring a new level of understanding or meaning to what we read.

The meaning of what we read is only partially dependent upon the words themselves. If everyone got the same meaning from the same print then we would not need lawyers, Bible scholars, or literary intellectuals to interpret the written words of others. Take this story for instance:

A woman was going to hire a new housekeeper. The homeowner speaks to the new employee, "My windows need washing. Do you clean windows?" The housekeeper replied, "I don't care to." The homeowner said that was fine and left it at that. When the homeowner got home the next afternoon she was shocked to see that all the windows were cleaned. When she asked the housekeeper, "Why did you clean the windows? I understood you to say you didn't care to do them." "I didn't care to do them," replied the housekeeper. "I am good at windows and I like cleaning them."

Clearly, what we have here is a failure to communicate! The homeowner's experience with the phrase "I don't care to" meant "I don't want to." The housekeeper's use of the phrase "I don't care to" meant "I don't mind." The words are the same in both instances, but the meaning exactly opposite. The difference lies totally in the experiential backgrounds of the two people having the conversation.

The effect is that meaning cannot lie totally in the words we read or say, but must also be partially constructed in our brains as we connect to what we already know, have experienced, and believe.

In a very real way this is what makes reading so messy. If there were only one way to call some words and then everyone know exactly what they meant, we could have written this book on a napkin. However, because reading involves thinking and thinking involves taking all the possible meanings of all the words and running them through a brain-based algorithm that weighs, categorizes, synthesizes, and then pairs and intertwines with preexisting knowledge and perceptions, well, it makes reading and understanding one of the most incredible feats people can accomplish. Yet, it is the most essential thing for people to have any semblance of freedom. If you cannot read on your own to determine what you believe, then you are left with people telling you what you believe. There is power in words and language. People who are trapped under governmental rule that does not allow freedom to obtain print, to become literate, or to speak to their beliefs live under crushing oppression.

Just as body language, tone, and context affect the way we understand what is said to us in person, there are devices that writers use to affect understanding in print. There is no way that an author can include all possible details about any given topic. The author has to make choices about what must be included and general expectations about what the reader may already know. Writers want to be understood just as people want to be understood when they speak (a possible exception might be politicians! ☺). Therefore, writers include devices that guide the reader as he or she constructs meaning from the print. Inferences are often derived from the diction (vocabulary) the writer uses. An author who uses the word *horrific* is telling you something more than one who uses the word *bad*. Likewise, when an author uses six sentences to describe the weather patterns of a particular land, but only one sentence to describe the type of currency used, readers know that the importance of weather has a much larger significance in the scope of the text. This constitutes another way that authors guide us toward using the words on the page, along with what we already know, to construct understanding and draw conclusions based on those understandings.

There are two ways here that readers can go awry as they read. One is to be so literal with the print that the only thing they consider is verbatim what the text says. That ignores that the writers cannot provide all the meaning that is needed for understanding and decision-making based on those words. The other way to go astray is to allow the gist of the print to be crushed by previous experiences (schema) the reader holds. If the print is overriding your own knowledge at too deep a level that is called "bottom-up processing"—the print crushes your own thinking and you have an overreliance on expressly what is said in the print. An overreliance on "top-down processing" means that you are discounting the actual print, preferring your own reality in your head. It is important for you to know that terminology as you must monitor your own balance of those two types of processes.

So, how do you police your own thinking to know how much of each process (top-down vs. bottom-up) you use? The amount of emphasis on each process is on a sliding scale as a general rule. Let's say you are reading a legal document that has great bearing on your financial well-being. You are going to want to rely more heavily on bottom-up processing, right? Yes. The exact words used, in the particular way they are used, and their use in the overall context is essential. There is never a time when you only use one process or the other. The idea is that you are aware that both types of processes are essential to understanding and that an overreliance on either one will cost you in terms of comprehension and certainly impact any decisions made on what you read.

Some general rules of thumb when making inferences from print would be:

1. Identify what the text says explicitly—avoid all distractors (opinions) and search for facts.

2. Think about what you already know.

3. Determine how what you read fits with what you already know, incorporating the new information.

4. Check your logic—is what you now think logical?

5. Put your conclusion or current belief after reading this piece into words.

6. Can you defend your stance based on the text and through the lens of your own knowledge?

While these general guidelines are numbered, the actual process is more recursive than linear in nature. You may have to revisit the actual facts in a piece more than once. You may decide after coming to a conclusion that your inference was biased based on your own experiences. Sometimes even after carefully determining all the above criteria, you may still get the feeling that you are guessing at what the author was really trying to communicate with you. This is why discussing a passage with others is so beneficial. It is why writing in response to reading helps us know what we think. It is through these processes that we become better at reasoning, better at thinking logically, and better at unlocking the meaning of what we read.

We have already talked about how formulating questions about a piece/chapter you are going to read really helps you read actively. Sometimes those questions are provided for you by your instructors. Just because a sentence ends with a question mark doesn't mean that all questions are created equal. A question can prompt for an answer that is **clearly divulged in the text**. The answer is right there in black and white. Other questions might cause you to have to **think** about what you've read and **then search** for more information in the text to be able to respond in an informed way. Yet other types of questions are directed at what you think completely **on your own**. These may happen after you have read a particular text so that you can become fluent at responding to text. The on-your-own types of questions could also happen prior to the reading to encourage you to draw from your own experiences to respond to the question. These types of questions may also be asked as you are reading so that you begin to assimilate the new information in what you already know. By carefully determining what kind of question you are being asked, you can more efficiently and accurately respond either orally or in writing. You should ask yourself: *What is the relationship of this question to how I find/develop the answer?*

- **CCSS.ELA-Literacy.CCRA.R.4** Interpret words and phrases as they are used in a text, including determining technical, connotative, and figurative meanings, and analyze how specific word choices shape meaning or tone.

- **CCSS.ELA-Literacy.CCRA.R.5** Analyze the structure of texts, including how specific sentences, paragraphs, and larger portions of the text (e.g., a section, chapter, scene, or stanza) relate to each other and the whole.

- **CCSS.ELA-Literacy.CCRA.R.6** Assess how point of view or purpose shapes the content and style of a text.

- **CCSS.ELA-Literacy.CCRA.R.7** Integrate and evaluate content presented in diverse media and formats, including visually and quantitatively, as well as in words.

How can I possibly know what the author is thinking or what he wants me to know?

You have likely spent the equivalent of a year of your life being asked to interpret, identify, draw conclusions about, and otherwise determine what this-that-or-the-other author is thinking. Many times that is referred to as the author's purpose for generating the writing. When someone writes something there is a purpose in mind. Either they want to tell you something factual (like in a textbook), they want to entertain you (stories, poems), or they want to persuade your thinking in some way by sharing their thoughts with you. Information-type books are nonfiction by nature. They tell you something. Authors organize the information in the best way to help readers make sense of something they want you to know. It is fairly straightforward to determine the central ideas or the main points the authors of information books make. They use headings, charts, graphs, bullet points, and other constructs to guide the reader to the most important bits of information or concepts. The challenge with information texts is understanding the concepts and determining how all the pieces fit together.

Expository writing moves in a straightforward way and is often arranged in some type of chronological order. Information-based writing does not have characters, setting, plot, or action that builds so you have to make your own predictions. Just preview the text first and then make predictions about the text. What do you think the text is about? If you find textbook reading to be less than interesting, you will have to find strategies for engaging with the text (preview, connect with prior knowledge, connect with personal experience, and visualize).

Expository writing does not have a beginning, middle, and ending so you must depend on headings to lead you. If you're having trouble comprehending the text, turn your headings into questions and after you read the sections under the heading, see if you can answer your questions. This strategy will also keep you engaged in the text and keep you from daydreaming.

Textbooks, articles, and online readings can have stilted or academic vocabulary and may not have a conversational style. Such text can be full of complicated vocabulary that you may have to figure out from context or look up in the dictionary or the glossary. When looking up a word, look in the glossary first; the dictionary may not contain specialized words unique to certain disciplines. You might find it helpful if you keep a word list. You'll find that your textbooks use repeated words and once you learn basic meanings, you will not have to consult the dictionary or glossary as much.

Make sure you allow yourself sufficient time to complete your reading. You may not want to read the text all at once to avoid daydreaming. You may want to break your reading into several ½-hour to 45-minute time slots. This may help you stay focused. In textbook reading, you may have a tendency to call words instead of comprehend the text. Think about how you typically read your assigned textbooks. Strong readers typically monitor for each of these as they read:

1. Am I aware of when I'm losing focus?
2. Do I know strategies for staying on track?
3. Did I turn the headings into questions and do I understand information under the headings?
4. Do I understand the vocabulary?
5. Have I allotted an adequate amount of time to read the text?

In other types of books/writings, the central ideas and themes are not as easily identified or understood. Have you ever tried to write the directions for tying your shoes? Tying your shoes is easy and you do it without thinking. However, when you try to put words together to explain what you are doing with the strings, you soon find that it reads like an extremely complicated process that very few people could actually do. Similar experiences include when you try reading the directions for putting together something you have purchased. For most of us the LAST thing we want to do is open the directions and read or try to follow the complex diagrams with parts labeled ''a'' or ''b'' and ''slot-this-or-that.'' Writers experience this same complication of language when they try to explain their thoughts. Instead of writing in short, declarative sentences, most writers tend to "wax poetic" or engage in complicated inferences to other works, use obscure vocabulary, and speak in analogies. Many times this leaves the reader with a "say what?" feeling after reading a passage.

The truth is that most people do want to be understood in what they are writing even if you want to scream "just say it" when you are trying to deconstruct a written passage. Authors use certain constructs to get their points across:

- Writers will compare and contrast ideas: "A lease-to-own house is just like an outright purchase in terms of paying taxes and insurance, but very different in terms of the types of loans and down payments that are required." Often, they will try to use a common analogy outside the topic to help you set up the comparison/contrast they are attempting to get you to make with the topic of the piece. The thinking is that if you can understand the common analogy, you will be more apt to understand the relationship the author is trying to set up with the real topic. Sometimes readers find these distracting—why are we reading about real estate when this paper/chapter is about biology? However, it is just these types of writing devices that readers need to look for. If you get in step with the way the author is trying to get your attention, you will find that you actually understand what they are trying to communicate. Underline these as you go. They will equal understanding.

- Sometimes writers will try to get you to understand with critical vocabulary—very descriptive language that carries deep meaning. Instead of saying someone was "unpleasant" to deal with the author might describe the person as "impossible, aggravating, exasperating, or infuriating." Look for high-impact words that indicate the author's passion. That's where the author's real thinking comes through. Don't read past/through word usage. Good authors are very deliberate in the words they use. The whole secret to understanding fact versus opinion in a piece is in the vocabulary. If someone is trying to persuade your thinking they will be very selective in the high-impact words they use. The best writers can do this with subtlety. They will lull you into a fact-based dialogue and start to sprinkle in some words that sway you—words that have more than one meaning (English is just chock-full of those), words that have emotional impact ("Those are fighting words, buddy!"), and words that move your thinking toward what they want you to believe. Oh, heck, just read a political speech. It's all there.

- When a speaker spends more time on one aspect of a topic than another, you intuitively know that the highlighted aspect is of key importance to the speaker. The same with writers. Note how much "time" the author spends on particular component of the topic. Are there elaborative explanations, substantial examples, or added effects like lists, bullet points, graphs, charts, or diagrams? The author is communicating to you what he or she considers to be of vital importance.

The first step is to say to yourself, "This person wants to tell me something." Then do some self-questioning as you read.

1. What does this author want me to know? (central ideas or themes)
2. What does this author want me to believe? (influences my thinking)
3. How is the author building the themes or ideas together to make a certain argument?

Mark or note each idea presented (1, 2, 3, . . .). Draw lines under the examples, justifications, and explanations provided by the author. If you take this one step further, you can move on into Text Annotation. Basically, that means you make notes in the book/on the article. For some people, writing down notes in a notebook just does not work for them. They have trouble connecting their written notes back to the reading or to the lecture/classroom experience. However, writing notes directly beside the reading helps some people keep the information tightly connected. And for those of us who lose notebooks like we do our shoes, this is a lifesaver. Worried about losing your textbook? Use a dollar bill as a bookmark. No one I know walks off and leaves money. Just the fact that you SLOW DOWN and THINK as you read means that you will automatically have better recall and understanding. The trick with Text Annotation is "what to write," so that it is actually useful to you.

1. Vocabulary is a must. Circle/highlight words that are keeping you from understanding the concepts. If there is a synonym for the word, draw a line and put the synonym in the margin so that as you reread for clarity you can easily

substitute the word. This works for words that are not discipline-specific (we call those academic vocabulary— the vocabulary of learning).

2. Discipline-specific vocabulary. These are not only words you have to understand while you are reading, but you must *remember* them as part of the content of the course. Most of the time these words are already marked for you in some way (bolded, italicized). Use context clues to note a brief definition of the words or look them up in the glossary of the book and jot down just enough so that when you see the word again, you know what it means.

3. If there are several parts of a process or a series of events that surround a happening of some sort, number them as you go. It is easier for your brain to reproduce a numbered list than a series of items that are not intuitively connected.

4. Just like visualization provides cues to aid your brain for recalling information, so does sketching pictures/ illustrations in the margin. If you can think about an idea, vocabulary word, essential concept enough to formulate an image of some sort that represents a big idea, then you are more likely to recognize it instantly when you revisit your notes.

5. As you are reading, you may say in your head, "I need to ask about this in class," however by the time class actually rolls around you can no longer recall what you wanted to ask or what component of the reading was unclear to you. If you do something as simple as drawing a question mark at those junctures in your reading, it will prompt you to pay close attention to the explanations shared in class or to ask about the concept.

6. Summarize in the margins. You will not remember word-for-word what the author says. You will remember your own words. If you take the time to restate the essential concepts, you will "own" them. Additionally, you will know you understand what the author has presented when you can restate the arguments or ideas and how the author makes the points.

A well-annotated text will allow you to study without the need to reread the chapters. To study from your annotated notes, cover the text and read your comments. Can you look up from the print and say aloud what you understand? This is a nice method of impressing information on your brain, as verbalizing will actually help encode the words in your mind and make them easier to recall. If you cannot restate the concepts, then uncover the text and read around the key information/terms. If you can talk yourself through the entire chapter, you can be assured the you are learning this material as actively as is humanly possible.

Part III

Cracking the Binding

We get reading assignments of 50 to 60 pages in multiple courses per week. How can I possibly get through that much reading when I have no time?

I mean seriously. What to do? You have this big stack of books, several syllabi stacked in a pile (or scattered, as the case may be), and a calendar that is blowing up. Be not afraid. As you "go bravely into that dark night" (that is called an *allusion*), you have to conquer the volume of reading by setting priorities. All reading assignments are not created equal.

First, determine which are serious reading assignments and which might in reality be optional. Look at a syllabus and think about the directives you were given in class. Did the professor make a believer out of you in terms of doing the reading? Most of the time they are telling you the truth and trying to help you be successful. Did you hear that the reading is essential either directly stated or emphatically implied? If you believe that the reading is going to make or break you when it comes to getting the grade you want (You want an A, right? Most certainly.), then put that textbook on top. It is a must. What you must do, you will do.

If the reading *seems* iffy—you are not *sure* if it is essential to your success, then put it in the *possible* pile. Be very attentive to the professor and the references made to the text. Keep your antennae up for these references when test-time is coming up. After the first test you should be able to move the book to the *for sure* pile, or possibly get in line at the bookstore for a huge $3 payday when you sell it back. If the professor is not using the required textbooks as essential learning components of the course (and shame on them if they are not), then you have to make the hard/smart call. The learning for that course is evidently supposed to happen *some other way* and the reading/textbooks are not essential. Move on.

By the third week in the semester, you should have a pretty solid feel for which reading assignments are actually *essential.* Do those. No debate, no drop-back-and-punt, no get-out-of-jail-free card for this. Essential means essential. Mark those readings with sticky-notes in your book. Put the date the chapter is due on a sticky-note and then put that note on the first page of the assigned chapter. There are times (true story) that students miss knowing that a reading assignment is due because they cannot find their syllabus, it is too much trouble to log onto Blackboard (insert course management system of your choice here), and someone is ordering pizza. Having the information in your face, so to speak, means you are well on your way to actually doing it.

Now you may still have this really intimidating stack of all that *must be read.* You open the book, determine how many pages are assigned, rethink your life, sigh, basically go through all of the seven stages of grief, and then focus your eyes on the title of the chapter. Stop. Why are you reading this? If you do not have a purpose then go play Frisbee. You are wasting your time. The chances of you remembering what you are going to read *passively* (without purposes) are not very good. Not at all. You have to discipline yourself to use some sort of active reading strategy that keeps your brain engaged in the reading. Someone should write a book with ideas for that!

Book in hand, strategy in place, brain engaged—you are ready to read. Are you lying down? Get up. If you don't, you will be asleep in three minutes. There are millions of people who take sleep aids when all they need to do is read a chapter in a textbook. Are you hungry? Thirsty? You will be in five minutes. Get a snack and something to drink so you don't have to get up and interrupt your work. Is your phone on? Yes, it is. At least turn it to vibrate. Television on? Your brain cannot keep up with reading and listening at the same time. You can sort of do it, and you may even have yourself convinced that you are actually good at multitasking, but your brain begs to differ. Do you have yourself convinced that you have ADHD, ADD, or some other type of attention problem? You might, you might not. Every single human being that needs to concentrate for extended periods of time has to train himself or herself to do so. And so what if you do have an attention problem? You still have to do the work. It might take you longer to develop the deep and extended time concentration levels you want and need, but you will find that everyone has something to overcome—their own mountains to climb, so to speak. Quitting is not an option.

Let's do some math. Some reading experts say that you should study three hours for every one hour of class. If you are take 15 hours a semester, then you are in class (face-to-face or online format) 15 hours a week. If you multiply those 15 hours by 3, you will see that studying and reading for 45 hours per week is what might be your optimum amount of effort. You have to be realistic and carve time out for this work. It may not, in reality, take you 45 hours per week to be successful in your courses. Maybe you are super smart, super organized, super motivated, super attentive and attendant in class, and cute to boot. That's all well and good. You still need to work.

If you are now thoroughly convinced that effort is your friend, then let's talk about some shortcuts to reading. You have your proposes clearly in mind and your active reading strategies clearly in hand. Those determine the way you read. You have to pay attention to how you need to pace the reading. *Skimming* a text involves letting the information "jump out at you." Your job is to be ready to catch it! You are actively noting chapter headings, subheadings, charts, graphs, images, any callout boxes, words in italics or bolded fonts, and basically all the things we call *text features.* Your mind is open, your notebook is open, your pen is flying across the book's pages making notes, underlining and otherwise noting the important parts. *Scanning* through a text (chapter, article, etc.) means that you are reading with an *end in mind.* You have a specific question or focused purpose to locate some explicitly stated information. If you are responding to a reading guide provided by your instructor, scanning is your best bet. If you are left to your own accord to get what you think the instructor wants you to get, then skimming is your friend.

It might be that in both skimming or scanning you have to train your eyes to go where your brain needs them to go. Your brain and your eyes have to work together in orchestrated perfection. Think of synchronized swimming. The effect only works when every single person is completely in sync with all others. If one person is off even slightly, you end up with a bunch of strangely attired wet people plastered in fake smiles. *Trackers* are great training tools for directing your eyes where you want them to fall, and also for maintaining the rate at which your eyes must move. You can use an index card or better yet, a credit card, your university identification card, or any piece of cardboard cut to size. It is best to start training with something that goes the width or almost the width of the printed page. Your goal is to keep reducing

Practice Creates Proficiency

Think about something that you're really good at (OK, if you chose sleeping or eating, think of something else). Most of you probably thought of the way in which you excel at a particular sport or the fact that you are a very skilled driver.* Whatever it is you are considering, you know what you're doing when it comes to _____. Now, think about how you became such a great . . . guitar player, let's say. For most people, being around a person who is learning a new instrument is one of the most unethical forms of torture. An unidentifiable tune filled with sour notes and the occasional expletive screamed by the "musician" does not make for very pleasurable background music. But alas, you were not concerned with the fact that your parents were banging their heads against the wall and your brother's ears were bleeding. You and "Mary Had a Little Lamb" kept pushing until it was right (well mostly). After a few more days of torture, you added "Twinkle Twinkle Little Star" to your repertoire and before you knew it, "Smoke on the Water" was child's play. It wasn't too far-fetched for you to be mistaken for the next Hendrix, except you put your strings on right-side up. Thankfully, mercifully, you were getting better with the ol' guitar.

As you've experienced time and again, if you expect to be good at anything, you have to do it. Thus comes the saying "practice makes perfect." Football players do not have three practices per day in the summer heat because the coaches are bored. Nobody would dare argue this. It's far too obvious that Olympians train daily for four years merely to have the opportunity to run one race lasting 10 seconds. We've seen it and we understand it. Why then do we not consider the same habitual training when it comes to our brains? Why do we think that we can sleep and watch TV all summer and then pick up a college-level textbook and run with it? If that's all we did all summer, we couldn't even literally run with it for too long. Cognitively speaking, just as with physical and emotional training, proficiency requires practice. We must train our brains to think well, to read well, to reason, to remember. Moreover, we must **practice** these behaviors to become adept at utilizing the skills. Studying material for a test will be beneficial for recalling the information for that test; however, it is also a crucial step in becoming a better test-taker and a better studier.

Additionally, it should be noted that the adage "practice makes perfect" is a bit misleading. The saying should more accurately go like "perfect practice makes perfect." You can put in hours of work digging a nice-sized hole. You can have the sweaty clothes and blistered hands

* Interesting side-note: Regardless of culture, age, sex, or experience, a common belief that ties all of us together is that individually, we all believe we are above-average drivers. That cannot possibly be the case . . .

to prove that you made quite the effort in removing the earth from its previous dwelling and relocating it to the pile adjacent to your newly formed void. The problem is if the hole was supposed to be on the other side of the street, all of your work was worthless. In fact, it was worse than useless because now you're tired and have blisters. Practicing is not the only key to yielding a quality product. Practicing the **right way** is just as important. Many students have some thoroughly engrained, very well-learned habits that are counterproductive. Perfect practice makes perfect. If you're going to dig the hole, you might as well make sure you're digging it in the right spot.

the size of the tracker until you can get the same speedy effect with a pencil or pen. That in itself speeds you along since you don't have to switch from tracker to pen to make notes, underline, or circle important ideas. Drag the tracker from the top of the page to the bottom, allowing your eyes to land on chunks of information at one time. Try to keep the pace of the movement of the tracker at a constant speed. It will astound you as to how much you will know at the end of a page using this method. It will be energy-consuming in terms of concentration so don't expect to fly through a chapter the way you can fly through a page. Your brain/concentration will wane. You will have to have a few breaks and time to organize your notes and thoughts before attacking the next page or section of the text.

There are times, woe unto us, that we must actually read whole paragraphs, pages, and sections of the book. That is determined by:

1. How complicated the concepts are.
2. How familiar or unfamiliar you are with the concepts.
3. The amount of emphasis put on this concept by your instructor.
4. How well you are doing in the class.

Complicated concepts are just that—complicated. It may actually take more than one reading for you to even begin to wrap your mind around what you need to learn. There is a reason universities don't just hand out diplomas on the corner as you drive by. You need to leave there knowing stuff. Many times students are asked to comprehend complicated concepts that it has taken their professors years to master. This is where the rubber meets the road and you find out if you can hack the tough learning to get the degree you want. You will not only have to read the required texts, but you will spend nights combing through anything you can get your hands on trying to learn this stuff. You will go to study groups, watch videos, and even go to the library to be able to concentrate.

There is one huge antidote to complicated concepts: experience. If you are *familiar* with the concepts because of some prior knowledge about the topic then you will grasp the learning so much more quickly and, likely, deeper than your peers. Maybe your high school physics teacher was awesome, your grandfather was a historian, or you have lived in an area of the world that gave you first-hand knowledge, experience, or exposure to the things you are studying. This will only work for you on those rare occasions that you have enough depth of understanding to put you ahead of the curve. Then, there is the assumption that what you learned actually helped you. Maybe you learned it differently or altogether wrong from the way it is being taught to you now. It is harder to relearn than to learn the first time. Do no pass go; do not collect $200. Savor those precious times when familiarity with the concepts helps you—they are sweet.

Learning to read is important. Learning to read your professor is priceless! If you find yourself getting frustrated because it does not seem to you that your prof is doing his or her job and not telling you what he or she wants. Think again. That, number 1, is a waste of time, and number 2, means you are not *hearing, seeing,* or *interpreting* the **code** they are most certainly communicating with you. Professors are creatures of habit like everyone else. They will fall into a "pattern" of behaviors in the way they teach, question, test, provide resources, and interact with students. Blindly ignoring those nuances is not a good idea. You will find it infinitely more interesting to study your professor when you are in class and taking notes, participating in projects, and in class discussions. Just like poker players, profs have "tells" or tics. I try to be very overt and exaggerated when I am about to get knee-deep into something I find fascinating and of major importance. My students can practically be in a coma and when my voice changes pitch as I slide into my "brilliant" lecture on one of my favorite topics or a particularly passionate speech atop my soapbox, suddenly pens are flying across pages and students are hanging on my every word. You have to listen for those changes in intonation. Also, note the amount of time profs spend on any particular topic. Time spent on a topic is an indicator of its importance. If a professor ever starts a sentence with "My personal research . . . ," or "I was involved in . . . ," you should write down every word possible. Professors will try to sell you on what they consider to be most important. Some will stand still and let the words soak in, or you might note others pacing excitedly when they are getting to what they consider "the good stuff." These are the billboards for communicating to you what you need to write down, read, study, and learn.

Ox in the ditch? We learned to play school (different than playing doctor) a long time ago. Your habits now drive your thinking. In high school, you may not have had to really buckle down until the grades hit the toilet and you were at risk of not getting to play your sport, losing the keys to your car, or (insert other punitive threat here). In college, by the time you come to the realization that you are in trouble, you are in trouble. Depending on how low your grades are, it may not be possible to pull them out in what is left of the 15 weeks of a semester. You have to do the math based on the syllabus—how many points possible for a/an (insert target grade of your choice here) and how many possible points are left in course. You may find yourself trying to solve for x as you determine what you would have to make on the final to average in with your current grade to achieve targeted final grade of your choice. If, however, you find that there is a Hail Mary to be had, then the *way you read* the assigned text takes on a whole new level of pursuit. You need to read, take notes, reread, overlearn, and pull out all the stops when melding your class notes and reading notes. It is also a good idea to show this new game plan to your professor, as it doesn't hurt if the ref is aware that a Hail Mary is coming his or her way.

Other considerations for handling the volume of reading:

- It's important to get in an area where you can concentrate, an area free from distractions. Leave friends, leave family, and study. Reading in the right environment really saves time getting in concentration mode. You should read in the same environment every day so you won't have to take time to adjust to a new environment.

- Reward yourself. After you finish a goal, reward yourself: Take a break and meet a friend; watch a television show; text a friend; get some ice cream; play a video game; get on Facebook or call a friend. One caveat: Do not get so lost in your reward that you do not return to your homework.

- Once you open your book, you should preview the text. Previewing for some students seems like extra work but it'll pay off in the end when you can locate the answers easier and you are more precise in comprehending the text. Look at headings, pictures, charts and graphs. Look at the first sentence in each paragraph. Just skim the text to find out the most important details. Previewing gives you two exposures to the text instead of one exposure from reading the text without previewing. Two exposures provide reinforcement and better comprehension.

- You don't read everything at the same rate so it's OK to read texts faster in the subjects in which you do well. It's equally OK to read texts in subjects you do not do well in slower. Whether fast or slow, make sure you're getting key ideas from every page. Remember not to move your lips when you read. Moving your lips causes you to slow down. Note that you may need to move your lips when you read difficult text and have to read it aloud so you can hear the text.

- How many times have you read a text and didn't understand it, and your instructor, teacher or professor told you to read it again and reread it until you understood it? Rereading is a good strategy if you only use it sparingly. If you do it repeatedly and still do not understand the material, it's likely you will get frustrated, particularly in the case of intense reading. You need another strategy. Use multiple strategies for comprehension. Turn headings into questions; pretend you're talking to a friend and "talk out" the passage; map out the author's thoughts and arguments, draw a line down your paper and write the main ideas in one column and your opinion in the other column. One strategy for comprehension may not work all the time.

- Use multiple strategies for vocabulary, too. Try to determine the meanings of words using context clues. Deducing meaning from surrounding words or sentences really reduces time. Reaching for the dictionary every time you encounter an unknown word is time-consuming. What if you encountered eight unfamiliar words in one paragraph? You would forget what you read with the interruptions from reaching for the dictionary that often. Use the dictionary or a glossary when you completely do not know the word and it is an essential word to understanding the sentence or passage.

- One of most time-consuming aspects of reading can be note-taking. Students write page after page of notes and before you know it, you have a book of notes! Paraphrase the text; in other words, summarize the text in your own words. Make your notes shorter than the original text. Reference page numbers so that you can go back to pages for clarification if needed. Take notes using abbreviations as if you are texting someone. Your notes do not have to make sense to anyone but you.

- Is the vocabulary difficult? If so, you might need to spend a little longer with the text applying strategies for figuring out words. Are you interested in the text? If not, you might need to spend a little longer with the text employing strategies for connecting with the text. Does the text have plenty of white space for you to write in the margins? Does the text have pictures, graphs, and headings for you to preview? If the text does not have these features, then you need time to figure out how you are going to attack the text, take notes, and create visuals to help you relate to and remember the information.

The average first-year college student reads between 250–300 words per minute for a text with average level readability. If you are reading below these rates, you could have trouble completing assignments in a timely manner. The goal is not the ability to read fast; the goal is to read fast with comprehension. If you just read fast, you're simply calling words and not comprehending the text. If you read with understanding, then you've actually comprehended the text quickly. So the question is, how can I read faster with comprehension? Here are tips for increasing your reading rate:

1. Are you reading every word? Stop it. Focus on ideas instead of words.

2. Read everything you can. The more you read, the better you'll get at reading.

3. Expand your fixations or chunking. Fixations are the number of words your eyes rest on as you read.

4. Make sure you locate the most important facts in the text and focus on these to help comprehend the text.

- **CCSS.ELA-Literacy.CCRA.R.2** Determine central ideas or themes of a text and analyze their development; summarize the key supporting details and ideas.

- **CCSS.ELA-Literacy.CCRA.R.5** Analyze the structure of texts, including how specific sentences, paragraphs, and larger portions of the text (e.g., a section, chapter, scene, or stanza) relate to each other and the whole.

- **CCSS.ELA-Literacy.CCRA.R.10** Read and comprehend complex literary and informational texts independently and proficiently.

How is the way I read a novel different than the way I read a textbook?

An overwhelming amount of your reading in college will be in the form of information text: textbooks, articles, documentaries, webpages, and research. You will need to read literary pieces in your English classes and other courses may require novels, short stories, and biographies that will require you know the difference between how you read a novel and how you attack the print in a textbook. The real answer to this question is to know the difference between *narrative literature* and *expository literature.* A novel, a short story, a play, or basically any writing that "tells a story" is narrative literature. It contains characters, plot, setting, time order, climax, conflict, and other elements. In addition, it has a beginning, middle, and ending. The beginning of the story usually describes the setting and introduces of characters. Some characters play major roles in the story and others have minor roles. They often have multiple points of view about the same incident. If there are a number of characters in a novel, you may have trouble keeping up with them and their different points of view. If this happens to you, just take notes. Write down the names of the characters, their identifying role in the book, such as daughter or carpenter or store-owner, write down their points of view, and their involvement in the story. It might also help you to draw a diagram for how people are related to one another, like a family tree. It is easy to be overwhelmed with too many characters and it may seem like you are reading the phone book (lots of characters, get it?).

Authors include details that describe characters or events in the story so the reader can create a mental picture. If you are good at visualizing, you may actually feel like you have "seen" the story as a movie in your head. This accounts for why we are often disappointed when we see a movie based on a book we have read. The movie has trouble living up the images we have built in our heads.

In addition, characters speak in dialect. If the dialect is unfamiliar to you, you might have to look up these words on the Internet. Similarly, novels often contain allusions to cultural events or objects. If these are unfamiliar, just look them up. Generally, narrative writing does not contain difficult vocabulary. In fact, novels often use abstract language, relaxed language, and language that appeals to our senses, so the vocabulary is easy to read. However, that can lead you into a trap as well: Words in literary passages carry heavy meaning. Fiction writers love to play with language so they will use words that have multiple meanings, and other literary devices like the following:

- **allegory**—the use of metaphors to substitute a more common idea or thing for a complex concept

- **allusion**—reference to a person, place, or thing that implies the reader already knows the reference

- **analogy**—tries to establish a relationship by pointing out similarities between two things or concepts

- **euphemisms**—the use of nicer words in place of more harsh ones

- **foreshadowing**—gentle hints the author gives you for how a story will unfold

- **imagery**—allows you to form mental images

- **irony**—implied meaning is different from literal meaning

- **metaphors**—words or phrases that allow us to know much about a person, place, event, etc., by direct alignment with something we already know

- **mood**—atmosphere the author sets to influence the reader's emotional reaction to a setting, characters, or incident

We also have to attend to the plot, conflict, theme, and time order in literary pieces. The plot builds as the action increases and occasionally there is foreshadowing of the outcome. The foreshadowing allows you to predict easily the event that is coming next. In the movies or on television, you have music and pictures to cue you in on what's coming up, but in novels and stories, you have to depend on words—very meaning-heavy words.

Narrative literature can move in chronological order but it can also move through flashbacks into the past or flash-forwards into the future in a single story. This can be confusing to the reader unless the reader looks at the story holistically and pieces the scenes together. Developing a timeline really helps.

Almost no professor is going to ask you to read a novel (literary story of some sort) unless they are going to ask you to DO SOMETHING WITH IT. Without exception they are going to want to know if you know the following:

- Do I understand the author's purpose for writing the novel?

- Do I understand all the main characters and their points of view?

- What is the theme (that is different from the storyline)?

- Can I describe the plot including the beginning, middle, and ending?

- Do I understand inferences in the novel?

- Do I understand all the ideas relating to culture?

- Can I follow the time order in the novel?

- What does an examination of the word choices the author makes tell me about?

- What is the author's worldview?

In other words, you cannot just know what happens or who did what. You have to read more words in fiction than you do in information print (like textbooks). You have to go more slowly (most of the time) because what may seem like a simple turn of phrase or event may make what happens next make no sense at all on the literal level, so you have to retrace your steps and figure out where you went offtrack. The good news is that narrative, literary reading is more like life—there are people, places, and things happen. The bad news is you have to see all this through whatever lens the author chooses. If the story is one-dimensional—literal meanings throughout, simple plot, simple characters, and predictable outcomes, well, you would trash that in any review. Want to know what you hate more than that? Didactic writing. Preachy, I will tell you what you think, I will tell you what you should do, presumptuous authors who treat you like you cannot think for yourself. So, don't be too quick to get frustrated with complex writing that is challenging, requires your full attention, and forces you to think in a way you may not have ever thought before.

The authors of these writings have the highest respect for you and your incredible brain.

Part of the challenge of reading and understanding all the nuances of good literature is knowing how to weave the meanings together as you go along. Whereas with nonfiction information books, the text itself makes the important parts pretty easy to distinguish. Authors and publishers use lists, graphs, diagrams, bold and italic fonts, headings and subheadings to aid readers as they try to take cues from the print itself. These text features are missing from fiction and literary works. In fact, you may find yourself thinking that the author deliberately wrote in some sort of secret code just to confound the meaning. Clever, complex writing may very well be like unraveling a puzzle, deconstructing a complicated algorithm, and trying to understand nuances of meanings that seem to be chameleon by nature. It is very easy to get frustrated and spun into a frenzy from the effort of not only making sense of what the author has written but also from trying to explain these layers of meaning to someone else.

One "high-utility" strategy is visualization. Visualizing is a useful tool in expository (information) text as well, but it really is a must for literary writing. Applying visualization when reading your textbooks means you are developing images that serve as cues to link information together. An example might be to think of a series of processes of some science concept that start with a broad approach, narrow to a small synthesis of just a few pieces of data, and then expand back out again to be generalized to a broader expanse. That was tough to follow, but if you think of the following image while learning those processes the image will trigger your recall of the sequence of what is happening:

In literary reading we use visualization to help us weave the story in our heads. If you use the descriptions that authors give you and force yourself to envision the characteristics of people in the story, you can recall those as you read. In your mind's eye, you know exactly what the protagonist (main character) looks like when he or she is happy, sad, angry, and confused. It's the same for the setting: The more details the author provides, the more vivid the images in your mind are. If you really get into this you will also smell what the characters smell ("Is that smoke?"), hear what they hear ("Wolf? Definitely, wolf!"), feel what they feel ("The ice was so cold it burned his skin"), see what they see, and taste what they taste. Allow yourself to include your senses as much as possible.

The next piece you are going to read is unlike most anything you have read before. You will need all the devices and strategies at your disposal to be able the answer the questions posed earlier in this chapter. Follow these directions to try your hand at visualization as a means of discovering the author's meaning.

1. Read this through the first time for the pleasure of the story. It is likely you will still have questions at the end.

2. Read through the second time marking all the parts of the story that prompt images or the connection to your senses (things you can hear, smell, taste, touch, see).

3. Write (or draw, if you prefer) a character sketch for each character in the story. Use the white space in the margins—stick figures are fine as they will denote height, weight, and other physical features as described in the story.

4. Put the story into your own words using your own understanding of what happened. Use this as a basis for discussion in class. Literature not worth talking about is pretty much not worth reading.

- **CCSS.ELA-Literacy.CCRA.R.3** Analyze how and why individuals, events, or ideas develop and interact over the course of a text.

- **CCSS.ELA-Literacy.CCRA.R.4** Interpret words and phrases as they are used in a text, including determining technical, connotative, and figurative meanings, and analyze how specific word choices shape meaning or tone.

My books are full of charts, graphs, callouts, and pictures with captions. It makes it go faster if I skip those and just read the paragraphs. Is that a good strategy?

With the increase in technology, we obtain information from a combination of print and symbols and have to rely on pictures, charts, graphs and other visuals for comprehension. Unless you have a photographic memory, it is impossible to categorize a large amount of items and written material in your head, so we use charts and graphs to compile information and show relationships.

Many textbooks have valuable information in the form of bars, charts, graphs, and other types of visuals. The purpose is to compile information. Textbooks use visuals to emphasize important information and to avoid repeating information in print. To ensure comprehension, it is important for students to get two exposures to important information in the text, one in print format and one in visual format. But our tendency is to skip these. To our eyes, these look like immediate and intense WORK and something extra to do. We are tempted not to look at study charts, graphs, and pictures but the truth is, visuals are really helpful when reading.

Charts, graphs, and pictures can help you preview the text to tell you what the text is about. The visuals summarize the most important parts of the text in symbol form; after all, authors would not put unimportant information in visuals. So if you have trouble distinguishing important information from unimportant information, look at the visuals. If it's in a visual, it's important.

Charts, graphs, and pictures can help clarify what you read. Visuals summarize the text, so if you are confused about material that you read and you have gaps in comprehension, take a look at the visuals. They may clear up any confusion.

You may want to take notes by using visuals, particularly if your professor goes too fast in lecture. Taking notes by using visuals is called mapping. Mapping is way of showing relationships among ideas in the text. Mapping involves clustering ideas and using visual representations to identify key details in a text.

Test Yourself: Can you tell what this passage is about by looking at the map?

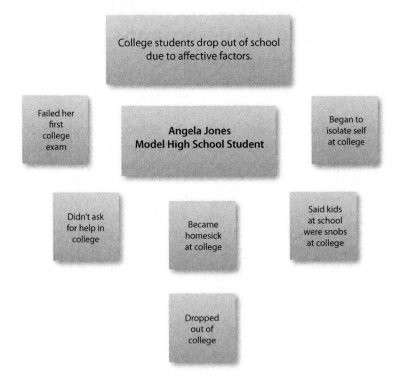

College students drop out of school due to affective factors.

Failed her first college exam

Angela Jones Model High School Student

Began to isolate self at college

Didn't ask for help in college

Became homesick at college

Said kids at school were snobs at college

Dropped out of college

Who or what is the subject of the map?

Why is the author writing this article?

Recap: So is skipping over visuals a good idea? Absolutely not. Graphs, charts, illustrations, and other visual representations are there specifically to aid comprehension. Visuals help summarize the text so that the text does not have to repeat emphasized ideas in print. You can get the main ideas from the text by looking at the visuals; that's why when you preview the text, you should always look at charts, graphs, and pictures. You can even take notes using visuals. It's a great way to summarize ideas and take down the important facts on paper during lecture or even when reading.

The next time you read complex text on unfamiliar topics, have little interest in the material, and find that you comprehend very little of it, try this: Turn every visual aid into a narrative and every narrative section to a visual aid of your own making. There is no way to convert narrative to image or image to narrative without understanding what you are reading.

- **CCSS.ELA-Literacy.CCRA.R.1** Read closely to determine what the text says explicitly and to make logical inferences from it; cite specific textual evidence when writing or speaking to support conclusions drawn from the text.

- **CCSS.ELA-Literacy.CCRA.R.2** Determine central ideas or themes of a text and analyze their development; summarize the key supporting details and ideas.

How do I find pleasure in reading when I hate it so much?

If you hate to read it is because you were taught to hate it. True story. Kelly Gallagher, in his book *Readicide: How Schools Are Killing Reading and What You Can Do About It,* defines "readicide" as "The systematic killing of the love of reading, often exacerbated by the inane, mind-numbing practices found in schools" (p. 2). It is very likely that you *loved* books when you started school. You liked to hold them, look at the pictures, and flip through the pages. It is also likely that you loved having people read to and with you. Very shortly thereafter (before noon in Kindergarten day one) you started to get this creepy feeling that they were about to turn you and books into adversaries. The words that sounded so incredible when your mom or dad read them to you soon became fodder for phonics. You were suddenly responsible for every sound in every word and any meaning that word had was simply a by-product. Every story was reduced to characters, settings, and hard, hard questions about the meanings of every single aspect of the book. It didn't take you long to learn that if you picked a book up you had better be ready to relentlessly demonstrate your skills just to get to read it.

A visit to the library, which in previous generations had been about choice and daydreaming about other times, people, and lands, became a pursuit of colored dots—and you dared not look at much less touch the books with dots outside your appointed color. You were a "yellow" and you should be interested in all dots yellow. If you tried to buck this system you were quickly excluded from pizza parties, recognition awards, and getting your name on the big chart in the hallway. Not only were you a yellow, you were not a very good yellow at that. The library became your first experience with a caste system and you didn't even have the vocabulary or concept development to understand the discrimination you deeply felt.

Those first experiences were likely followed up with years of workbooks and exercises that had you identify the main idea until you developed a mental twitch when you saw a book coming your way. And textbooks? Would it be possible for them to be any worse? Dry, short sentences that repeat the same things over and over, accented by enough diagrams, charts, and graphs to choke a horse. I am hoping your experiences were better, but it is very likely you have never learned anything from a book. Given any other option it is likely that you chose it over actually reading an assigned chapter in a textbook. Instead of learning that books hold treasures and incite intellectual spurs of understanding, you learned that they are to be avoided at all costs.

Just like the word *pleasure* implies, there is something about the mixture of clever language and the images we build in our heads while reading that allows us to *feel* something. The black squiggles arranged on white paper can cause you to have a physical reaction. When simply reading transitions into an actual *conversation* between you and the writer, a bond begins to form. You start to think and do "inside-your-head talking" almost alongside the author. You anticipate the next reaction, the next event, and depending on what type of writing it is, how it will end. You will catch yourself using the same vernacular as the writer, picking up slang, and certainly growing your vocabulary. For novels, you want to find a character that you can relate to. You will immediately look for a character that is good looking, physically powerful, exhibits courage, is terribly clever and, of course, is an exact replica of you! Once you lock onto your alter ego, you will be cheering for him, feeling his pain, flinching as he flinches, and possibly, crying when he cries. Most of us can understand a physical reaction from watching a movie or video, but from one-dimensional black squiggles? And it feels good on top of that? We could talk all day about the pleasure of reading, but that won't convince you. Your habits and attitudes were set years ago and I am just coming off as a book nerd. I smile. Best kept secret ever.

Let's try another angle. When is the last time you got better at something you don't do? That's a backward way of saying, you only get better at things you actually do. Because we are human, we avoid what we hate to do. The more you avoid reading the more you stay stuck where you are. That would be fine if your future as an adult and productive member of society didn't depend in a great part on your literacy levels. There is one simple fix for this situation. And only one. You have to learn to trust books again. You have to consume literary and information writings as you learned to eat broccoli (substitute the veggie you learned to eat and now enjoy). One bite at a time. You have to learn to become critical consumers of print. All writing is not created equal and, just like food, you learn to develop a taste for it. However, if you don't take the first bite with a willingness to enhance your palate, you will forever be struggling with only knowing what you are told and believing what others want you to believe.

It is your attitude that makes the difference between learning to eat new foods or forever living on mac 'n' cheese and pizza. Whereas with foods there are those to help guide us—restaurants with quality ingredients, cookbooks, television shows that feature ad nauseam chefs, cakes, cook-offs, and cuisine from around the world. It is a bit harder to get good recommendations for quality reading material. Book stores like Barnes and Noble and Amazon include "reader recommendation lists" and customer reviews to help guide readers to make good decisions about what they want to read. Some connoisseurs of reading follow favorite authors, reading everything they write. Some follow genres—all manners of fiction and nonfiction including biographies, graphic novels, mysteries, romance novels, self-help books, and books written to provide information on every imaginable place, people, and event. For most of us, getting started includes trying new dishes (books/writers) and finding out what we like through trial and error.

The Immature Thinker

Immaturity. We've all experienced its consequences. Truthfully, each of us at some point in our lives has been the culprit—engaging in some adolescent escapade that we now regret. It is usually not until we experience the actions of an immature person that we realize how foolish some of our own decisions may have been. Playing mailbox baseball with your buddies is hilarious—paying for a new mailbox every other week (just to have it filled with bills) is not so funny. Now that we're older and wiser, we look at those young whippersnappers and think, "why don't they just grow up." The truth is, most of us have to go through those awkward stages of bad decision making as part of our quest toward adulthood. On the road of immaturity, we encounter situations which require us to alter our course. We used to save our birthday money, our allowance, and whatever cash we could get from mowing lawns or selling tiny cups of lemonade to purchase some new gadget or toy. As we grew older, we (hopefully) have realized that we

(continues)

(continued)

must make sacrifices in terms of what we **want** to be able to buy what we **need**. The ability to make these decisions is just one characteristic of a person who is on the right path to maturity.

Before you think that this is getting much too philosophical, and at the expense of sounding far too much like your parents or your dear grand pappy, it is important to note that there is a point to all of this maturity talk. You see, our brains operate in a very similar way when it comes to thinking and learning. The majority of the physical makeup of our brains is devoted to keeping us alive. There are specialized centers devoted to controlling and interpreting the information for our senses. There are portions that control our vital organ functioning, our language, and our memory. We usually do not have to think if we are hungry or tired, if we need to run away or stay, or if we are happy or sad. With all of these responsibilities (plus countless others), there isn't much space left for thinking and learning. In fact, humans are not very good at thinking. It doesn't come naturally to our brains and therefore, often takes a back seat. We must take preemptive measures to combat any stimuli that may serve as distractors to our thinking. You probably remember the high stakes testing toward the end of the school year growing up. Your teachers likely stressed the importance of getting enough sleep and eating a good breakfast. They were simply trying to eliminate the possibility of another brain function impeding your ability to think well on the test and therefore save them from the wrath of the state department if you performed poorly.

The point is that thinking is **hard**. We have to purposefully devote concerted time and energy toward learning and thoughtfulness because our brains do not revert to those processes out of habit. We have **immature** brains in this aspect. When we were younger, it never crossed our egocentric little minds that it would be much more beneficial to put our money into a CD or savings account. All we could think about was buying that silly thing we wanted (that we used a couple of times and either broke or threw away). As the stakes increased, we realized that we had to start taking care of some things that wouldn't just take care of themselves. We saved for a car, paid for our gas and insurance, and our cell phone that we cannot live without. Now we have to pay rent and pinch pennies to pay for college. Instead of buying a video game, we buy a new vacuum cleaner. The funny thing is, we're just as excited to open the box and try it out. As the stakes increase for our education, we must make the same decisions. This means that we have to take the time necessary to focus on new material and we must eliminate any distractors that are battling for our attention. As we make these beneficial decisions, our brains are no longer such inexperienced thinkers. They will indeed, **mature**. But, just as if we had never began taking care of ourselves financially and socially, if we do not make accommodations to become better learners, we would still be at mommy and daddy's house watching cartoons in our pajamas. And that, my friend, is not attractive.

If you asked a thousand people who are self-proclaimed reada-holics why they love to read, you would likely get almost as many different reasons. However, most of them would boil down to this—we do not read to find out about others, we read to find out about ourselves. Most of our lives are spent with each one of us trying to figure out exactly who we are. Are we brave? Are we kind? Are we worthy? We use whatever yardsticks we have to measure those things, however, the events of our lives define what we do know about ourselves. What if there was a way to know how we would react if put in thousands of situations that define the measure of a person? There is. Books allow us to relive the past and explore a future that does not yet, or may never, exist. We, through the lives of those we encounter in books, get to learn about ourselves. And there is something intensely pleasurable about being intellectually stimulated as you are drawn into a world where you hang on every word and feel nostalgic when the last word is read and the book is closed.

It's called pleasure. What are you hungry for?

- **CCSS.ELA-Literacy.CCRA.R.1** Read closely to determine what the text says explicitly and to make logical inferences from it; cite specific textual evidence when writing or speaking to support conclusions drawn from the text.

- **CCSS.ELA-Literacy.CCRA.R.4** Interpret words and phrases as they are used in a text, including determining technical, connotative, and figurative meanings, and analyze how specific word choices shape meaning or tone.

How can I make myself be interested in what I read?

I'm sure you have had a reading assignment that you've found less than interesting. No matter how hard you tried, you just couldn't seem to focus on your reading. Perhaps you tried to read your assignment and found yourself daydreaming and still looking at the same paragraph 30 minutes after you started reading. Or perhaps you tried to finish the reading and found yourself at the end of numerous pages without knowing a single detail. Your first impulse is to fling the book across the room, but you figure that this won't really solve anything. What should you do when you get stuck like this? You have to read and your brain is screaming, "I do not CARE" with every molecule of its cauliflower-looking self.

First, guess what? This happens to every single human ALL the time! You are not special in this dilemma. So, how can some people read a thick chapter called "Ancient Greece and Rome: Society and Politics" without any problem and you dread it like a root canal? It the same reason some people love Brussels sprouts and some people hurl when they look at them. It's a matter of personal taste. For most of us it has to do with our backgrounds and personal experiences. It is also a matter of what is culturally relevant to you and valued among your family and friends. If your grandfather is a historian and you grew up seeing his books and listening to his stories, it is very likely you will value what he valued. You will find interest just in *knowing* more about things that he loved. Therefore, you will push yourself to read material that others might find infinitely boring—you are genuinely self-motivated to read and understand. If no one in your family held a passion for science, you might find reading biology or chemistry the most grueling exercise in the world. Same person. Same set of abilities. Totally different results in reading.

Your personal taste for a type of reading dictates your self-motivation. In other words, if you don't consciously or subconsciously send a signal to your brain to "get in the game," then it is very likely that you will read passively. Which is just as good as not reading at all. Reading is a brain function. No brain, no reading. The real challenge is when you try to read something that is rather repulsive to you and you either send a very weak signal alerting your brain to attend, or you just blunder right in without a purpose, plan, or way to stay engaged. Turning that around is a matter of habit and discipline. Did you get the memo? You are an adult now and you are expected to have self-discipline. Bummer, huh? Success in reading and comprehending—actually *learning something*—is totally on you. Not the professor. Not the fact that the book may suck. Not any type of self-diagnosed disability label you might try to wear. You. Just you.

So, pull up those bootstraps and let's figure out how to discipline yourself into reading and understanding text that bores the hair off your head. First, let's take a look at the monster we hope to slay.

Preview the Text

You have heard this a bazillion times, but if you preview the text, you'll get a general idea of what the text is about. It's like gathering fragments of the text in your mind before you actually read the text. Then, as you read, the text becomes clearer. You get more information that leads to a complete picture and once you have a complete picture, you have comprehension. To preview a text you go on a scouting expedition:

1. How many pages are we talking about? Your dread factor will go up or down based on this.

2. Is it dense reading with paragraphs that go on and on, or is it broken up by pictures, tables, and illustrations? Our first plan is to read the paragraphs and skip all those "space takers." Wrong. You will find more information, more quickly, and more succinctly in those features than in pages and pages of paragraphs. Think about it—what you hate is the forest of words, sentences, and dense paragraphs. Learn to like the pictures, tables, and illustrations; often they are quick summaries of what it took the author many words to say in print.

3. How can I use the chapter headings as announcements of "coming attractions?" Authors work hard to figure out how to tell you something. Authors try to put information in chunks and then give those chunks names. You should be able to go through a 30-page chapter, make a list of

headings (leaving some blank space in your notebook) and then have a complete skeleton of the chapter. The sweet thing about doing this is that you then "own" the information. Previously uninteresting volumes of blah, blah, blah actually make sense. Sweet!

4. What other neat tricks do these clever authors put in place? Many publishers require potential authors to submit a prospectus of the textbook they are going to write. Every chapter will be squashed down to just a paragraph or so that cuts to the chase to explain what the chapter will entail. This is like the "trailer" of a newly released movie. It contains the gist of the plot and works hard to grab your attention without giving away too much. Trailers leave you wanting more. The print equivalent is the "introduction" to the chapter. Read the introduction. The authors assume you will and then jump in like you know what to expect. Do your brain a favor and read the introduction. The text needs to connect to something you already know and the introduction provides that conduit.

5. Are there still other things to look for, you ask? Indeed. Just in case you read a whole chapter and still have no idea what just happened, the authors provide chapter summaries. You will find those at the end of a chapter along with questions the authors think might help you understand. You may prefer to have your fingernails jerked out one-by-one while listening to Rosanne Barr sing the national anthem set to loop ad infinitum than either read or attempt to respond to those questions. You have bigger fish to fry. Do not labor over those questions unless you have been specifically directed to do so by your professor—or in the rare case that you actually find that type of exercise helpful and you enjoy pain. A better use of your time might be to look for **bold** type or words in *italics.* Many authors assume we will not read closely and try to give you quick tips (a flashing marquee, so to speak) to get your attention. Make use of their assumption and note the flashing lights!

Connect

Now that you know what you are up against in terms of volume and complexity of the text you need to read, you are ready to alert your brain that it is on active duty. You are not a blank slate or an empty vessel waiting to be filled. For your brain to make sense of the world around you it has to constantly weave connections between and among cells. Those connections are called dendrites, and the number you have dictates the amount of information you retain and can retrieve. Think of it as your own personal "Google" search engine. When you ask your brain to connect to what you know about a person, place, event, or even a word, it does an amazing sweep of over one million billion cells and connections to report to you what you already have stored there on that particular topic. You don't get a print option, but you do get flooded with every possible connection you have with that topic. All that is wasted if you have not alerted your brain to make that information available to you. It has to be deliberate and you have to develop the mental discipline to go through the process.

What are some ways you can connect with the text? You know when you meet someone at a cookout at a friend's house and you are stuck with talking to him at least for a short time ? Once you both agree that it is a nice day and your friend's backyard is nice, you are pretty much just standing there awkwardly looking at each other. You have to actually feign interest as you form another question. Could be, "Where are you from?" or "What's your major?" The point is that you search some elements of existence that people have in common until you find some way to connect. "Where are you from?" could lead to finding out that you and this guy lived in the same county at the same time but attended different schools. It might be that you have cousins that live there or it is your uncle's favorite hunting ground. The same types of connections could be made by finding out that you are both in engineering, only you are in electrical engineering and he is going to be a civil engineer. Now you have some common professors to complain about. You asked questions until you found a connection. Until that connection is made the weather and the backyard are all you have in common. Not a very interesting conversation and certainly not one in which you make a new friend or enjoy a visit with a cool person. It is the same with an unknown text. Until you find a way to connect with it there will be no conversation—no free exchange of ideas and thoughts. It will just be some flat words that cannot find a place to stick in your brain. Sounds like a waste of time to me.

There are basically three ways to get your brain to connect with text:

- What personal experience with or knowledge of the topic do you have? You may have heard the expression "jog your memory." That means to force your retrieval system to respond to/connect with certain words, terms, or names. When you first read the title of the chapter/article/challenging text you need to read, force yourself to jog your memory regarding that topic. Either make a mental list or quickly jot down all the things you know about the topic. Your brain will have received the signal it needs to attend to this new information. Your first and most powerful connection will be fully in place when this happens.

- What have you ever read or seen or heard (think media) about this topic? You may never have been to outer space and lived among alien beings, but via a novel or movie you have built background information about those things that you have stored and can retrieve. We know many things about the past, (dinosaurs are examples) that we have not personally experienced. Yet we know dinosaur names, what they ate, and can speculate as to how they became extinct. If you jog your memory for personal experience and come up with nada then ask yourself, "Have I ever read a book, seen a movie, or in some second-hand way learned something about this topic?" Make a mental list or write down those connections. You can't trust this information quite as much. You will be relying on what someone else has told you (like a novel or an unreliable website). Still, the information is there in your brain and you can use this reading opportunity to reinforce what you thought you knew or adjust what you know about the topic based on this new and more reliable (hopefully) information source.

- The third way listed here might or might not be easy to get to, but in some cases it may be all you have left to use as a connection. How does the text you are trying to read connect with your worldview? Did you know you have one? You have belief systems in place regarding society, freedom, justice, patriotism, government, religion, human rights, and many other abstract constructs. The way you view those constructs colors your view of the world and how it should run. There are some topics that require you to know what you think about something in order to respond to it or even learn more about it. These might include culturally controversial topics like abortion, legalizing marijuana, the death penalty, or assisted suicide for terminally ill patients. Your views of these topics must be called into play for you to connect with the information you are going to read. These connections usually require you to form full statements that summarize your beliefs on these types of topics. You can (and should) adjust those as you work your way through the reading, but trying to read about them as though you are a blank slate with no held beliefs will leave you just that, blank.

Be Busy

You have given the text a good look and know what to expect. You have figured out what you already know or believe about the topic(s) and have made all the mental connections possible about what you are going to read. Still not highly motivated? Adjust your expectations. Reading is work. How often do you get all giddy about hard work? You do it because you have to. You personally benefit from the effort or otherwise you wouldn't do it. You earn money, you fulfill your self-directed obligations to church, community, humanity, or you get some sort of "warm fuzzy" feeling from the work. But you do not do it "just because." Reading something that is not a passion for you is like work. You approach it the way you do your job: you have agreed to do certain things for a certain amount of time each day in return for a certain compensation. You keep your end of the bargain by showing up with a good attitude and accomplishing the tasks to the best of your ability and then you get the reward in the form of money. If you approach reading your assigned texts that way, you will find your instructor or professor has made you the same deal. Show up with a good attitude, do the work and the return on your efforts will show up in your grades. Reading is work. Just do it. (Sorry Nike, I really had to say that).

The work part of reading is keeping your brain in the game. To do that you have to be accomplishing something as you read. Just "calling the words" silently in your head does not mean your brain is keeping up with anything. You need to be collecting, noting, scribing, and basically tearing that text apart as you read. That's the busy part. Even if you are still not intrinsically interested in the topic after all these efforts, you should be interested in the benefits of comprehending it—the payoff of your grade and your better understanding of some part of the world. Your brain will reward you with some endorphins for your efforts. It turns out that your brain appreciates being used for real work. Get yourself settled in a straight-backed chair (no comfy recliner for reading—sorry), at a well-lighted table replete with pens, pencils, sticky notes, and a pad of paper. Roll up your sleeves, turn your phone to vibrate, turn off your music, tell your roommate to buzz off and work at reading what you need to read. A plan for how you will mark, write, note, and collect needs to be in place before you begin. Then work your plan. Interest is little more than an adjusted attitude. Consider yourself adjusted!

Give it a Go!

Spit-shine that brand new attitude by learning a new strategy and then applying it to a passage that has the potential to bore you socks off!

Dialectical Note-Taking

Dialectical note-taking is a way of connecting to the text through taking notes. The word *dialectical* comes from the Greek word *dialektos,* which means conversation, speech or discussion. That is exactly what you do with the text in dialectical note-taking; you discuss and converse. Using a double entry format, dialectical note-taking helps you read critically and reflectively. If you reflect on the reading, you internalize the text, which leads to greater comprehension. Additionally, it allows you to connect with the text. This is important if you are reading a text you find boring. This type of interaction with print allows you to have something well thought-out to say about the text during class discussion. Everyone hates the feeling of being put on the spot when the professor calls on you in class and you don't know the answer. This is a great perk if you are awarded participation points for the amount of talking you do in class. It is also a great monitoring tool. It helps you keep track of your reading in a focused way that keeps your mind from wandering and daydreams at bay.

How To

To begin dialectical note-taking, draw a line down the center of your page and label the left column "Notes" and the right column "Connections." The Notes column contains the most important information in the text, such as what you would include in a summary. You don't have to make complete sentences, but make them clear enough to understand when you go back to them for the midterm or final exam. Paraphrase the text. Don't write everything down; abbreviate when appropriate. Go paragraph by paragraph and write the most important details.

The Connections section contains what you *think* about your notes in the Notes section. For literary text you could disagree with the author, write down unfamiliar vocabulary words, provide a comment to support the author's assertion, cite a personal experience or prior knowledge, ask a question, indicate that you don't understand an idea, discuss the author's point of view, discuss an author's bias or how the author forms his or her argument. For information text, you could draw a connection to prior knowledge, establish a cause/effect relationship, indicate the need for further research ("find this"-type comments), and formulate questions that clarify the concepts. The contents of this Connections section are not summary statements. Summary statements should go in your Notes section.

This is what the information provided so far might look like using dialectical note-taking:

Notes	Connections
Dialectical note-taking—thorough way to take notes	Wow, I need this. It sounds like a lot of work and time-consuming but it has great benefits.
Two columns—Notes and Connections	Do you have to have the same number of notes as you do observations?
Promotes reflection and critical thinking.	
Helps connect with the boring or unfamiliar. Helps readers monitor the text.	Might help me get through my Western Civ reading.

You do not have to have an equal number of comments for your Connections section as you do your Notes section, but you should have an observation every time you change a thought in your notes. If you do your dialectical note-taking correctly, you should be able to understand what the chapter is about by looking at your dialectical note-taking diagram and you shouldn't have to reread the text for tests. In fact, you should be able to take your notes from the left side of the page and turn them into questions to prepare for exams.

Now you can daydream about an A grade on your next test. Pretty sweet.

At first the process is slow and time-consuming, but with enough practice, it becomes faster and automatic. The benefits are you become a thorough note-taker, you can make yourself pay attention to what you are reading, and when you have waded through the text you will know what you read. Quite a payoff for a bit of discipline as you read.

Part IV

Hitting the Right Note

How can I take notes and listen at the same time?

You were likely never taught how to take notes. And even if you were, it was a lock-step process whereby a teacher put some stuff on the board and you wrote it down. Voilà, notes. Only you wrote every word that was displayed and there was no room or prompting for your own understanding or thoughts. You may as well have been handed a printed page with all the information. In fact, you may have been given those handouts, as teachers knew you didn't know how to take notes yourself. You have heard the old adage about giving someone fish versus teaching someone to fish? This applies here.

You're frantically trying to take notes while your professor is moving on to the next thought. You've raised your hand several times and asked him or her to repeat the information, but it's still not enough time to write things down. What do you do? When lecture consists of unfamiliar material, it's hard to take notes and listen at the same time. One of the keys is developing skills to focus on the main ideas during lecture; these skills involve good listening strategies and good note-taking strategies.

How many times have you had a professor who went on and on about a single detail? You felt your eyes getting heavy and you slouched down in your seat to get comfortable and before long, you noticed you were dozing. You may have missed key information while you were dozing and you frantically tried to focus on what your professor was saying but you were completely lost. Has that happened to you? If so, you need practice in being an active listener. Here are effective listening strategies for classroom lecture:

- Make sure you get plenty of rest the night before a lecture.

- Face the professor and sit up in your seat. This will help you to stay attentive instead of falling asleep.

- Focus on what the professor says. Don't think about what you will eat for lunch, other homework, or what you will do after class.

- Avoid external distractions. In the classroom, do not sit near the door or near the window. These are places where students get the most distracted.

- Let the professor go at his or her own pace. Don't rush the speaker for details. Listen to the professor's complete thought. He or she may be going in a totally different direction from what you thought.

- When the professor digresses, take this time to summarize important information that he/she said previously.

So, now you are in a college classroom and someone is standing there talking to you like he expects you to write it down. It is true that while many professors assign readings for each class meeting, they may or may not ever reference it. It is also true that while many professors may assign readings, your tests will likely come from lectures. As you learn to "play college" like you learned to "play school" in K–12, you begin to be able to discern what is expected from you in terms of reading, taking notes, and studying for exams. In many cases, *your class notes make or break your grade*. Knowing that you must be active with note-taking from the moment the prof starts talking until (thankfully) he stops will change the way you behave in class. You cannot mildly take notes. They won't be worth the paper used to write on. Note-taking is an active process with an endgame in mind. Your notes should be your custom-designed document of the content of the course that you must learn. Your studying and learning are aided by the quality of your notes.

You may find yourself thinking as you slump down in your seat at the beginning of class, "OK, show pony. Let's see whatcha got!" That demeanor will have to end if you are going to be engaged and develop notes that are actually helpful. The first step in taking notes is listening. You may believe yourself to have poor listening skills. We hear it all the time. You likely do have poor or underdeveloped listening skills. There is only one way to turn that around: Grow better listening skills. You must be aware of any of your behaviors and habits that inhibit good listening.

It may sound too basic to even mention, but you have to prepare to listen. Eat a snack before class so that a drop in blood sugar doesn't make you feel sleepy. Get enough sleep before class so that you are actually not sleep-deprived. Dress in layers in case the room is hot—it is hard to sweat and listen, sweat and think, or sweat and aggressively attend to what is being done in class. Sit close to the front of the room. Your concentration will wane the more distractions there are between you and the speaker. Your concentration will be short-circuited when you have to strain too long to hear the speaker. Keep your eyes on the speaker at all times. Until you make this a habit, tally the number of times you make eye contact with the professor during the lecture. When it becomes automatic and you see how much this pays off in terms of listening and taking notes, you will no long need to keep track of this.

To enhance your listening skills, learn to lay your troubles down outside the door of the classroom. Do a mental exercise whereby you run through a quick list of all the troubles on your mind and decide that for the next hour (or 2 or 3 hours, as the case may be) you will not try to solve those problems. You will not run through past conversations in your head, not try to think about what you are going to say to someone, and not worry. You are going to mentally leave these concerns outside the classroom door. Unless you are a terribly blessed person they will still be waiting for you when you exit the room and will climb right back up on your shoulders. However, trying to solve them during a class is actually *adding* to your problems, as now you have a lecture that has gone by like the wind and is gone forever. Adults have to learn to compartmentalize so that they have the mental fortitude to decide when and how (or if) they will worry about problems. If you are going to listen and think enough in class to take usable notes, you have to clear your mind for that period of time. We all have problems. It is just that some of us decide to work toward answers and others decide to worry. One gets you where you want to go and the other makes you sad and eats away at you. Emotion and worry will keep you from learning, which will cause you more emotion and worry due to failing grades. Lay them down so that you can focus.

We are going to assume at this time that you have grown your listening skills. But what about your professor's *speaking skills*? Perhaps your first language and your professor's first language are not the same. Now, you are not only having to listen and concentrate, but you feel like you are also functioning as an interpreter. The professor might do all sorts of things that impact your listening and note-taking, such as:

- Speaking too quickly
- Speaking too slowly

- Losing train-of-thought frequently

- Talking in circles

- Chicken walking (stories, anecdotes, and extraneous information)

- Not being prepared for lecture

- Failing to use any type of visual aid (PowerPoint, video, graphs, charts, illustrations)

Now that you know tips for active listening, let's work on listening for key points. To help you focus in on the key ideas your professor will discuss, you should read the material in advance. Your syllabus tells you what your professor will be covering from one week to the next. Even if he or she does not require you to read the chapter, you might consider reading the chapter and taking notes before your lecture. You will already be familiar with most of the concepts, ideas, and vocabulary, and it will be easier to take notes in class. You can at least do a quick *preview* of the assigned text first. Concentrate on the headings and how the headings are organized. Take note of any pictures, graphs, and other visuals. If there are chapter introductions and chapter summaries, you'll want to read those, too.

Another quick way to prepare for a lecture is to take notes in your book by annotating. The mark of a good student is a messy book filled with handwritten notes and sticky-notes. When you first begin to annotate a text, you may do excessive underlining in the text. A good annotation uses a *variety* of markings and marginal notes consisting of summary statements. For example, you may:

O	Place a circle around the key ideas.
_____	Underline any explanations of concepts that are very good.
?	Place a question mark next to material you do not understand.
O	Place a circle around unfamiliar vocabulary.
1,2,3	Write numbers next to information in a list.
[ ]	Place brackets around possible test questions.

Use Texting Abbreviations (ex, bc, wo).

Write marginal notes dealing with possible test questions, summary statements, or notes to ask in class.

Now that you've annotated the text, you're ready for lecture. During the lecture, you need to take additional notes. Remember, you don't want to be encumbered by minor details during class lecture or you might get bored. Focus on the most important points of the lecture so that you can be an active participant and get a full picture of the lecture; don't get offtrack. In a philosophy class, if you're discussing "If there is a God, then why is there evil?" then you would perhaps write down definitions of God and evil, any kind of background associated with the topic, any kind of modern-day theories associated with the topic, and other relevant information related to the topic. You would not take notes when the professor digresses from the topic. Because you annotated prior to the lecture, you can relax a little because you are already familiar with the material and already know the main points. In fact, you may look for clarification of unfamiliar vocabulary and concepts or material you did not understand when you annotated the text and ask questions. If the lecture is still moving fast, you may want to draw pictorial representations of ideas called *concept cards*. If you were discussing the sun's rays a concept drawing could look like the picture of a sun. If you are talking about someone being wealthy, then you could draw a picture of dollar signs. We are talking about quick and meaningful illustrations , ones that instantly bring to mind a concept, term, or other important learning.

How can you listen and take notes at the same time? By reading the chapter and annotating prior to the lecture, employing good listening strategies and focusing on the main points during lecture. You'll find that for even the most boring lecture, these strategies work so that you won't get rushed or frustrated.

You may have been assuming that your scattered notes were all your fault. However, you can write things down only as logically and linearly as they are told to you. It could be that the person speaking is not giving you much to work with. If that happens then you have to work harder to make it all make sense. You will need:

- Stronger notes from the reading,

- More research on your own to understand complex concepts,

- Connections to other students (prior and current) who have had the class,

- Any information/resources that your professor might have put in a course management system (like Blackboard) for you, and

- Visits with the professor or TA to ask for assistance.

Let's say that your professor is doing a pretty good job with the lectures. What do you specifically need to do to take good notes now that you are plugged in (listening), psyched up (actively engaged), and prepared to be an active participant in class? Here are some tips:

1. The pages you write on need to be constructed so as to help you organize the information.

2. Checkout the Cornell Note-taking System. Briefly stated, on the right side of page you write down all the important parts of the lecture. On the left side of page, you go back and put any terms, hot topics, and essentials you need to find again quickly. You can purchase paper already divided like this, or just draw a line about 3 inches from the left margin line on any ruled paper.

3. Listen for *emphasis* in the speaker's voice and watch for *body language* that indicates something important is being said. You may note a pause or deliberate eye-contact from the professor to signify that something of consequence has been said.

4. When you sense that kind of stress on a statement, you need to try to write it down verbatim. Otherwise, paraphrase the lecture content and put it in your own words.

5. Write down any references to webpages or other resources.

6. Write down formulas and lists or steps to something.

7. The value of writing down the information on a PowerPoint slide is that, even though the PowerPoint presentation may be in the course management system (like Blackboard), the explanation the professor provides will NOT be available later. If you write down the information on the slide (abbreviated as needed), then you can help contextualize that information with what the professor is saying as the information is displayed.

8. Sharpen your skills at noting the important information. You will have note-taking overkill going on if you try to script the entire lecture. And, the chances of you going back through tons and tons of notes are not very good. You may think you are going to rewrite your notes so you can just go into "autopilot" mode in class and write everything down.

Zoning out won't help you learn, understand, or remember. And, you are not going to go back and rewrite notes. Not that it is a bad thing to do, but with the volume of life going on with you, you won't have time except in extreme circumstances. Bully for you if you do, but don't put your eggs in that basket. Take good, clear, organized notes the first time through. Then you have something to study.

9. Rite the way u text. There r mny ways 2 b quik w notes & move on b4 the next note bc yr prof is moving on. TG2BT.

10. If you know how to write in cursive, do that instead of printing. **You can write more quickly in cursive. And your hand won't hurt.**

11. Leave plenty of white space on the page so that you can go back to add notes from reading, other resources, or to use while studying for an exam.

12. Need some practice keeping pace? Sit yourself down in front of the evening news. National or local, your call. Grab a pen and a pad of paper and take notes for 30 solid minutes. Your list should align with the television station's webpage of the major news stories of the day. Compare your notes with the webpage for accuracy and focus on the important aspects of the story. Do that a few times and you *will* increase your listening skills, your note-taking skills, and your concentration skills. And, you will know more about what is going on in your community and the world.

- **CCSS.ELA-Literacy.CCRA.R.7** Integrate and evaluate content presented in diverse media and formats, including visually and quantitatively, as well as in words.

- **CCSS.ELA-Literacy.CCRA.R.8** Delineate and evaluate the argument and specific claims in a text, including the validity of the reasoning as well as the relevance and sufficiency of the evidence.

- **CCSS.ELA-Literacy.CCRA.R.9** Analyze how two or more texts address similar themes or topics in order to build knowledge or to compare the approaches the authors take.

I highlight the important parts when I read. Isn't that good enough?

Perhaps it is the restriction of not getting to write in textbooks for so many years in elementary, middle, and high schools, but knowing that you own a book and can write, draw, or highlight to your heart's content may be very satisfying to you. All that is good and well until you realize you may actually need to make those marks mean something to you when you get around to learning from that book. You may be tempted to highlight important information as you read. Highlighting is little more than a "promise never kept." Typically, we think, "This is important so I will highlight it so that I can find it when I come back to learn it." News bulletin: You are not coming back. You will feel that you have read this and you got what you could when you read it. Taking notes, either in the margin, on paper, or electronically is a far better way of gathering important information. People usually revisit notes, reorganize

Image © Tatiana Popova, 2013. Used under license from Shutterstock, Inc.

notes, and rewrite notes. These are the times to use color. You can use multiple colors to discern different types of information. Make your notes visually stimulating. When you recall the information, you will actually remember what color it was in your notes.

Think of the text you are trying to read as a roadway. Recall the curviest, most mountainous road you have ever driven or ridden upon. While your goal is to get from point A to point B in the quickest possible method (we are always in a hurry, right?) and you want to keep pushing the gas pedal, there are times on the road when you have to touch the breaks or risk wrecking, tumbling over into a ravine, or losing control of the vehicle. Good readers behave the same way with text. There are times (straightaways) where you can pick up speed (skimming/scanning for key information) and there are times (sharp curves) when you have to slow it down (rereading confusing points) or risk wrecking (no comprehension). Therefore, when you say it "slows you down" to take notes, realize that this might actually be a good thing because it keeps you on the road (so to speak) with good comprehension. Very much like having to chew before you swallow food, you need to "grind up" some information

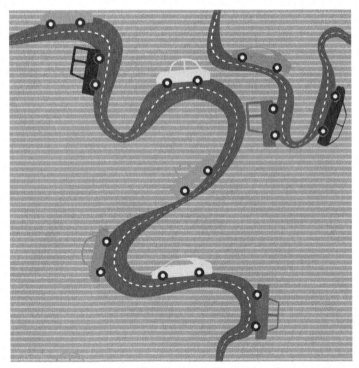

Image © Elena Kazanskaya, 2013. Used under license from Shutterstock, Inc.

before you are able to ingest it. If you use a highlighter as a turbo-booster for your reading whereby you slide that transparent pastel ink at lightening speed over what you are very quickly and without reflection deciding is important, you may actually be assuring that you won't get where you are trying to go (understanding what you are reading).

Put your highlighter down and grab a pen or pencil. You might start by circling or underlining key words and jotting connections you have to the reading in the white space on the pages. Now comes the time to put on the breaks (slow down) for any dangerous curves (confusing concepts or terminology) and stay the course. Rookies make the mistake of making too many notes. They are not yet critical consumers of print and, before they know it, they have pretty much rewritten the book in a notebook. Just like the pages of a textbook painted yellow with a highlighter, a notebook that includes too much information is likely not going to be of much use to you. Remember, your notebook you use for your assigned readings is just one of at least two you will need to keep going; the other one is your notebook you use for lecture/class notes. There is a whole section in this book regarding note-taking, so we won't go into specifics here other than to say that writing sentences straight from the book is not what we envision when we suggest you take notes as you read.

Notes from Reading

Your goal is to make a "cheat-sheet" or "one-pager" of information that is key to understanding what you read. Both names are misnomers, as we are neither encouraging you to actually cheat with the cheat-sheet, nor is the "one-pager" usually only one page long. The point is that you have a named plan (not some general notion) for how you will read and chronicle the information as you read. You write down the most important ideas in a text. Your brain does not care if you write your notes in the margin directly on the book or on a notepad, computer screen, or portable electronic device. Try it different ways and see what works for you. For some people it helps to write in the book, then transfer that information and expand upon it in a notebook, and then to type it into an electronic format that is organized and searchable. The multiple layers of exposure to the information in that example are part of a process called *overlearning*. Overlearning is spawned by rote memorization when writing or reading the same information over and over again. This works for many people but it doesn't work for everyone. There is no guide or magic wand to tell you which works for you and when (if at all) it works for you. You have to know how you learn. Once you have determined the best way to take notes then you can make that a staple in your strategy arsenal.

A "cheat-sheet"/"one-pager" would include the following:

- Major headings—shorten and personalize them in your own words, if necessary

- Summary sentence from the introduction

- Bold or italicized vocabulary that is key or new to you

- Key points from any graphs or illustrations

- Any questions you have that keep you from understanding what you are reading

- Summary sentence from the end-of-chapter summary

Now is the time you navigate the curvy reading road. Read the headings and at least the first paragraph underneath the headings with care. Determine if you get the idea. If yes, then skim or scan the rest of the paragraphs until the next heading. Fish out any bold or italicized words and any definitions in your own words. If you did not get the idea from the heading and first paragraph, then slow down and read the whole section more carefully. Make heavier notes and pause to "search your desktop" (aka your brain) to see if you can make any connections to prior learning or experiences. If you don't understand it at this point, you need to jot down some questions to ask in class or figure out as you continue to read. Rinse and repeat until all assigned pages are read. Use highlighters (yes, you can pick them back up) to color-code your notes: one color for major headings; second color for key words and vocabulary; third color for questions you still need answered; and continue until you have a quick system for finding information on your one-pager. This page(s) goes to class with you. If you have left white space, you can fill in more details from the lecture/class discussion. If not, you will want to take a separate set of notes and then make it a high priority to rewrite or in some way combine the information. All of this is easier with electronic notes. You can use a word processing program or any number of apps for your laptop, iPad, or other hand-held device. It is a really good idea to print these as well. Losing all your notes from a semester's work is tantamount to an electronic "fire" that destroys all your hard work.

Your one-pager might take any number of forms and still serve you nicely. It is likely that you have been taught to do outlines a few hundred times. Outlines work if you are very organized, get the giggles out of using Roman numerals, and think in a linear fashion. If you process a bit more globally, you might want to use rectangle, circles, and other shapes to design your own graphic organizer. For the Plain Janes among you, the old 1, 2, 3, etc., is perfect. The tech-savvy folks will want to take a look at two of the top-rated software note-taking applications, Evernote™ and OneNote™.

Evernote™ is a free computer program and device application that allows you to put everything in one place. You can include notes, pictures, documents, video clips, and audio files in this program and the best news is that you can sync with multiple devices (laptop, handhelds) so that you have access to your files wherever you go. Another great feature of this application is that you can get the add-on (still free) called Evernote Web Clipper™ that allows you to bookmark and annotate Internet sites you need. There are extra features that do require a paid subscription ($45 per year at the time of publication of this book), but the basics here are sweet in terms of supporting people who are collecting and organizing volumes of information.

OneNote™ is part of Microsoft's Office suite but is sold separately ($69 at the time of the publication of this book). The really cool thing about OneNote™ is that it looks like a 3-ring binder with tabs on the screen. You can add other files within each tab, copy and paste files, include video and audio, and it is easy to use. It provides apps for both iPhone and iPad.

Want to go old-school? Millions of learners swear by flashcards. They come in many colors and sizes, and you even have the option of a sticky-note feature. If you like the tactile feeling of moving the cards as you write and then reread (again and again) then it might be that these are for you. Go through your notes, either from your book or your notebook, and use 3 × 5 cards to record facts, concepts, and any vocabulary you need to learn. This makes quizzing yourself on the content very easy. Reading these and reciting them as you go through the cards provides the repetition needed for overlearning. Overlearning is the ultimate fluency on any subject. Reading or reciting the cards aloud involves more senses and makes it easier to recall the information. In the car for long periods of time? Read the notes into a recorder or your phone and play them back as you drive. Try to anticipate what you are saying next and finish your own sentences or thoughts. These are the types of *rehearsals* that imprint on the brain and further develop neuronal pathways that aid information retrieval.

Then after all this, how do you *know* that you *know* what you need to *know?* The big secret here is that you cannot retell what you do not understand. Maybe too many negatives there. Let's try that again: If you can retell or summarize the information, you know it. Summarizing as a skill/strategy reared its head when you were in the third or fourth grade. You likely hated it immediately. You were to take tons of stuff and reduce it to just a few sentences. Somewhere along the way, too much focus was put on learning how to do summarizing and not enough on the *why* of summarizing. Truly, without the *why,* the *how* doesn't make much difference because you are not going to do it as long as you live in a (relatively) free world. If you stop and put what you read in your own words (*summarizing*) as you are reading, then your notes will reflect your understanding of the content. Try doing this at the end of each major chunk of text or by major heading. If you summarize your thinking right then and write it down, you will have written your own "superhighway" to going back to these notes and comprehending the concepts.

How to Use Summarizing as a Means of Active Reading

A summary allows you to take key ideas from the text and put them in your own words so that it makes sense to you. It takes authors many more words to explain a concept than you actually need. When you selectively reduce the number of words, you provide your brain with an active way to make sense of what you are reading. Writing a summary is a good way to measure comprehension. If you can write or tell what you read in summary form, then you have comprehended the text.

Chapter 20

I want to sound intelligent when I talk in class. How do I do that?

Have you ever responded to a question the professor asked, when you finally got the courage to speak, and learned you were totally wrong? Have you ever known the answer to a question your professor asked and you didn't respond because you thought you might sound stupid? Have you ever raised your hand in class and when the professor acknowledged you, everyone turned to look at you and you forgot what you were going to say? These are embarrassing situations for most students. In almost every class, there seems to be a few students who are *not* shy about raising their hands and volunteering answers. These students discuss freely among peers, dialogue with the professor, and seem to know the answers to nearly everything. They appear to be smarter than everyone else in the class. They appear so confident. What is the difference between you and them? Nothing. It helps to know that all students are in the same boat—you are all there to learn and nobody knows *all* the answers. But some students are affected by peer pressure more than other students. And maybe you are one of those folks who are completely happy being quiet, savoring your thoughts. Maybe you are content hearing the professor drone on like the teacher from Charlie Brown. Maybe you aren't paying attention because you are on Facebook. Like it or not, you are going to be expected to ask questions, provide answers, and share your ideas and thoughts with peers in class (so get off of Facebook—but make sure you log out first; we don't want any funny business when your roommate borrows your laptop later). Many courses are set up so that some points are given for class participation. This is a painful thought for you if you are rather shy or quiet by nature.

There are a couple of ways to get in front of this. If your hesitation is due to being shy or the fear of speaking in front of others, then you need to help yourself find a comfort zone. Start with the most "friendly" class you have. A friendly class might be one with a small number of students. It can be very intimidating to speak up in a Psychology 100 course with 150 other students. Or, a friendly class might be one where you like and enjoy the instructor or in some way relate to the instructor. A friendly class might also be one in which you have witnessed others students participate, make mistakes, and realize that the instructor is very kind to students. If you do not have a habit of raising your hand to ask or answering questions, you need a good experience to boost your confidence. Once you know which class you find most comfortable, then you have to do the work to be ready. The best shield you have to guard you against feeling stressed about talking (asking questions or contributing) is being prepared for class.

You need to read the assignment in advance and make detailed, organized notes. Evaluate the text critically and anticipate what the instructor might ask in a class discussion. Thirty minutes before class **reread** your notes. Take your book to class. Be in class a few minutes early. Sit toward the front of the class. And never, ever, ever take your eyes off the instructor. You can take notes with a pen or use technology, but you have to be very disciplined not to check your e-mail or see what is going on with Facebook or ESPN. Your behaviors send signals to your instructor, your peers, and, most importantly, to your brain. You are in "professional student learning mode." Sit up straight and look interested. Truly. Every so often, when you know the instructor is pleased with himself with a joke he made, you smile or laugh too. Here is a keeper: When you learn to read your professor and know when she is particularly pleased with herself for saying some brilliant thing, tilt your head (right or left, doesn't matter), smile slightly, and nod while making eye contact with the prof. You have just acknowledged that she is as brilliant as she thinks she is. Score!

Once you get these behaviors in place, you are on your way to feeling confident as you dialogue freely with the professor and other students. You will soon realize that you do not have to have the right answer all the time or have the full conclusion worked out in your mind before you speak. You will realize the purpose of participating in class is to exchange ideas and build a repertoire of diverse ideas together as a class. You will find your voice and learn to like your voice as others respond to your thoughts.

During class, you have your sheet of critical responses (notes) that you wrote earlier. Consult these as your instructor initiates class discussions. In addition, make real-life connections with what the author, the professor, or a classmate is saying and share these thoughts and ideas. Make sure you *listen* carefully to the flow of ideas. If you are thinking about what you are going to say next, you may miss out on an important turn in the conversation. If you are not able to follow the line of conversation, pose a question, "I didn't understand why . . . ," or ask for further elaboration of a thought, or ask an opinion, "What did you think about this?" What you will find very quickly is that you were not the only student in the class with the same question. Ask your classmates or your professor to give examples. You paid for this opportunity so exercise your right to understand.

Still not feeling it? Then you might try an even friendlier format: study groups. If you have not had experience discussing in class, you may need a small group initially to gain confidence and experience in discussing. The student composition of your study group should be those students you feel most comfortable with in class. Small groups help you to engage in real conversation. Unlike studying alone, group members switch subjects with different thoughts and require you to follow the flow of the conversation, forcing you to listen to thoughts and changing conversations. Small groups will also help address reading content. If you are not certain about a portion of reading, then ask questions and clarify confusing points through group conversation. Another benefit of forming small groups is it will engage you in a diversity of opinions. You have the advantage of finding out other opinions before the real class. As you listen to others' opinions, you can strengthen your own opinion and anticipate counterarguments or find out why your opinion is not the best solution. Finally, small groups will help you get used to your classmates and gain friends in the class. It's always easier to speak aloud if you have familiar faces and kind friends around you. You may rotate your small groups eventually to include others in the class.

These tips are a great way to get extra points for participation. Remember, the more often you speak in class, the easier it will become. One way to prep for a class discussion is to have your thoughts, comments, and questions *preplanned*. Coding the assigned reading can help you do just that. There are many reasons and many ways to code text. For the purposes of this experience, use the following codes to prepare for a class discussion on the passage called "Unexplained Disappearances."

- **CCSS.ELA-Literacy.CCRA.R.7** Integrate and evaluate content presented in diverse media and formats, including visually and quantitatively, as well as in words.

- **CCSS.ELA-Literacy.CCRA.R.8** Delineate and evaluate the argument and specific claims in a text, including the validity of the reasoning as well as the relevance and sufficiency of the evidence.

- **CCSS.ELA-Literacy.CCRA.R.9** Analyze how two or more texts address similar themes or topics in order to build knowledge or to compare the approaches the authors take.

Part V

Word Herders

Why is it that I can learn specific science words or words in other disciplines, but I am constantly running into big words I don't know when I just read?

The English language is a complex conglomeration of words borrowed or stolen from many other languages. Spelling, pronunciations, and meanings follow vague patterns that are also impacted by the languages where the words originated. There are vocabulary words specific to certain disciplines such as biology, history, or mathematics, and there are words we use for learning called *academic words*. Some examples of academic words include *research, analysis, theory, policy,* and *variable.* Vocabulary development is a lifelong quest and no, putting them in a list and memorizing them is not how your brain learns new words.

We don't think much about the size of our vocabularies until we try to read something important and get stuck because the meaning of the words is unknown. Worse yet is when we are trying desperately to tell someone something in speech or print and we cannot find the words to give the exact meaning we need to relay. A strong and expanded vocabulary is key to successfully reading with meaning and writing with clarity.

"If I never see another list of vocabulary words in my life it will be too soon!" Have you ever said that? You have certainly thought it. While there are some components of memorization to learning new words, committing the words and meanings to memory is a useless task unless the words are connected to learning. In other words, your brain does not care to keep track of bits of information that are not connected to anything else. It will allow this to happen on a temporary basis (short-term memory), but as you have found from your past experiences, once those words have been used for whatever purpose you intended—usually a test—they fade away. Quickly.

So, if words are hard to learn and they don't stay with us, why bother? If as few as 5 percent of the words in a passage are words you do not know, you can pretty much forget understanding what the text says. The writing will feel vague to you and meaningless. Your time and energy is too valuable to be spent beating your head against the vocab wall, trying to squeeze deep meaning out of surface words within a text. Having a poor vocabulary will impact the rest of the reading skills you need to be successful in college and career. Unknown words or word meanings will slow your reading speed to a crawl. Since your brain needs new information "at a clip" it will discontinue trying to weave together meaning because the input (words you are reading) is coming in too slowly for it to process and make sense of it.

Learning new words takes too much time and too much effort for them to be a flyby exercise. What will serve you best is to learn how to learn new words in a way that keeps them readily available for your use, whether you see them in print, speak them, hear them, or use them yourself in your own writing. Developing a powerful and expanded vocabulary is doable. It is also hard work. That is the bad news. Now for two bits of good news: (1) vocabulary development requires just two things; and (2) there is a reciprocal relationship between vocabulary growth and comprehension growth both in reading and writing.

First, if you want to grow your vocabulary, you need to figure out how to learn the words as deeply as possible; you need repeated experiences with the words to ensure they are well-connected to learning; and that you have had enough repetition with the words to shift from short-term to long-term memory. The word-list method might have given you some repetition if writing things five or more times helps you, but it does little for the type of repetition needed to internalize new words and completely leaves out depth of word knowledge. To really know a word forever—in any context and through either receptive (reading, listening) or expressive (writing, speaking) means—you need to know much more than the definition. The definition of a word is the first step but not nearly enough for your brain to connect it to other learning/information.

- What is the origin of the word (where did the English language steal it from)?

- What part of speech can the word represent (English is famous for using the same words as nouns and verbs)?

- In what context might you see the word?

- Does it have more than one meaning?

- Is it composed of more than one morpheme (smallest unit of meaning—affixes are examples of this)?

- Are there any synonyms of the word?

- Are there antonyms of the word?

- Is the word plural or singular?

- Does the word have negative or positive connotations?

- Is there something I already know about this word that I can connect to?

- Is there an image that I can visualize that helps me "see" this word?

- Can I look at the word and immediately explain what it means in context in my own words?

That's a start. I encourage students to overlearn challenging words. Deliberately use them a minimum of five times a day until they flow fluently from your lips. This provides the stimulus for the second aspect of learning new words: repetition. You need to interact with the words you want to learn in any many ways and as many times as possible.

- Start with saying the words aloud, followed by as much information as you can possibly remember about each word.

- Write the words with "information chunks" about the words beside each one. Then rewrite them in categories. By synthesizing the words you help your brain put them into categories and make them easier to retrieve.

- Switch from paper and pencil or pen to using colored highlighters or ink to make key words "pop" on the paper. Code the words by color, making more refined categories. Categories might include: like parts of speech, plurals/ singulars, positive/negative, origin of word, context where words are most often found, and words that invoke images.

- Go high-tech. Enter the words and their information chunks of meanings into programs like VisualTheasurus.com, online dictionaries, or electronic flash card programs.

- Go old-school and put the words on one side of a flash card and the meanings on the other side. Put the words in different piles based on categories you develop. Use different colored index cards to represent different categories. Your brain wants you to help it know where to put these words so that you can access them on-demand.

More good news. Your brain likes to learn new words. It is one of the reasons that literate people play word games daily. Crossword puzzles, anagrams, hink-pinks, alliteration and rhyming games, acrostics, palindromes, puns, and rebuses are all types of wordplay that people *enjoy.* And each and every one of those serves to grow weak vocabularies into stronger ones. Scoot over tired, old lay-down-and-die words. A new tantalizing, invigorating, and formidable vocabulary is moving in!

Not all terms from science or other specific disciplines are easy and not all academic words are hard. However, it is usually easier for us to make connections to new words once we understand the main concept. For example, if you are learning about the bones of the body, then the words that name those bones are easier to learn in the context of how the skeletal system is organized. With academic words there is no relationship advantage—the words occur randomly and while context can help, many times you have few if any cues as to what the words might mean.

Learning to be critical in your analysis of challenging vocabulary is a good first step to becoming the word wizard with the expansive vocabulary you need for college and career. Earlier you were provided with a list of criteria that help determine the type of word and what a word might mean. Use the grid below to respond to those criteria using unknown words you find in the next passage.

- **CCSS.ELA-Literacy.CCRA.R.4** Interpret words and phrases as they are used in a text, including determining technical, connotative, and figurative meanings, and analyze how specific word choices shape meaning or tone.

Crossword? You mean "crossNERD?" How in the world could playing word games make me more literate?

So, your grandpa never met a *New York Times* Crossword Puzzle he didn't dive into, huh? The old fellow knew what was going on. Did your grandpa ever read any of the clues aloud, or ask you or another family member if they knew a six-letter word for "remember"? It is *recall* by the way. When grandpa involved anyone else in the search for a needed word, the activity shifted from a solitary effort to a socially interactive game of wordplay. Just by throwing Pops a word, you crossed over into a social multiple-player event that likely spawned more conversation, even if it was just a hearty "thank-you." Turns out that crossword puzzles and other types of wordplay games do way more for you than give you and your grandpa a way to pass the morning.

With the advancement of technology, it could be that even Pops has moved from paper-and-pencil crossword puzzles to interactive word games on his phone, iPad, or other handheld device. Whatever the venue, our brains benefit from playing with words. Neuronal pathways are carved that aid in the quick location of bits of information in the brain. We know that people who are avid readers and enjoy word games are less likely to develop Alzheimer's. What wordplay and reading offers the brain is parallel to the benefits of walking for the body. Also, like walking, wordplay feels good and is habit forming. Oh, yeah, and it's fun. Heck, Dr. Seuss got hooked and made a fortune out of rhyming words! Cats and hats, and Sams and hams all worked out really well for him.

Maybe you got into Words with Friends or Scrabble on your phone or iPad. If you did fall in love with one of these games or a similar type of word game, then you discovered what we word lovers already know: it's pure entertainment. Playing word games allows you to think about words in ways you rarely do. You learn to do quick "run-throughs" of your brain in which you command it to find a very particular word, sound, or meaning. Each time you search and recover one of those, you get quicker and more accurate at doing this. These are brain workout equivalents of push-ups, 5k runs, and Ironman cross-training, only you do not sweat or feel sore afterward. Cool. You get all the endorphins and none of the sprains or pulled muscles. One other nice side effect of wordplay is that you can be actively engaged in one part of your brain while the part that needs a break zones into this space where time is suspended and a relaxation settles upon you. Are you ever shocked that you have been playing for so long? Seems like you just started the game? Yep. Best time-travel ever.

People who aspire to be corporate giants study those who have reached those pinnacles. People who want to be leaders read books about leadership, attend conferences, and go to great lengths to hear great leaders talk about what they do and how they do it. Pick any other aspiration and what we do is study those who are where we want to be. It is the same for being literate and scholarly. You need to exhibit the same behaviors as those who are word and language savvy. Having a great command of language is an asset regardless of your chosen life-path. They engage in wordplay. They are intrigued by words and language. They never miss an opportunity to make or appreciate a good pun or play on words. In other words, language use in our culture is a mark of intelligence. Truly, there may not be one point difference in IQ between someone who exhibits savvy language use and someone who rarely speaks, but the *perception* in our society is that the silent person *might* be smart, but we *know* (based on our cultural bias) that the person who has a command of language is very smart. You might refer to this as behaving your way to success in language use. Observe what those who have a great command of language do. They keep their language skills sharp the same way that athletes keep their bodies in perfect working condition: they practice. They develop a love of not only the game (sports or words) but also a love for the practice that pushes them to the best they can be at whatever it is they are targeting.

Remember how much fun riddles were when you were young? Truly, they don't even have to be funny for a 6-year-old to bend over double with giggles. What you are about to see demonstrated will work with just about any topic. This example is pretty low-level, so you might consider how you can step it up a notch. The process is the same.

Do a mind map of any word. Put the target word in the center and then branch out from there with other words that are in some way connected to the word in the center.

Let's start with word *cat.* We drop the first sound—in this case the first sound is /c/. That leaves "at."

Now, list all the words you can think of that start with "at." Your list might look like this:

attack	attic
attention	attire
atmosphere	attended
atomic	athletic
atom	attitude

Then you construct your riddle:

What does every feline have? A cattitude.

Ok, you see what I did there? The first sound you dropped (/c/) was added back to one of the words that begin with "at."

One more time:

What is at the top of every cat's abode? A cattic!

No joke (get the pun?), this is the very last one:

How do you lead a herd of cats? First, you have to get their cattention!

Knock yourself out and develop a few riddles of your own. Keep in mind that to make your riddles funny and make sense, you have to develop a word list that starts with the letters after the first *sound* in the target word—not just the first letter. Below is an example list of the cat words from the graphic above. The first sounds are indicated in red.

paw	awake, award, aware, away, awesome
mouse	out, outrun, output, outlaw
claw	awake, award, aware, away, awesome
litter	itch, italics, itinerary
scratch	see the "at" list above
purr	urine, urology, urban
fur	urine, urology, urban

Note that the words *cat* and *scratch* will generate the same list of "at" words. Same thing for the "aw" words listed for *paw* and *claw.* And ditto for *purr* and *fur.* Not every word will either make sense or be funny. That is where your cleverness comes into play. Try this with some more abstract terms to make either political comments or comments on society. Some riddles are so clever that you start to laugh then it hits you what the riddle really means. Pow. There is power in words. Get it? I cannot stop myself!

• **CCSS.ELA-Literacy.CCRA.R.4** Interpret words and phrases as they are used in a text, including determining technical, connotative, and figurative meanings, and analyze how specific word choices shape meaning or tone.

A synonym, an antonym, and a homonym all walk into a bar . . . nah, not really. However, how can I keep all of these things straight and how can they help me have a better command of language?

We all learned the proper names for these word anomalies in elementary school. We understand how to identify them and maybe a little bit about why that matters. The real surprise is that a full and mature recognition of the value of how these quirky relationships between words work is essential to a commanding vocabulary. And guess who wins the most arguments, debates, wars, and rounds of *Wheel*? The people with a strong command of language and a deep understanding of how it works. True dat.

There are over a million words in the English language. Much of the language is begged, borrowed, and stolen from other languages, both modern and ancient. Tomes are written just to categorize and help people make sense of this galaxy of words. The purpose of learning to make those words work for you is the expression of ideas. Most people believe that we *think in language.* Ideas are formulated in language. The human condition is that we want to be understood. Having a strong command of language and the conventions of language help us make our point, succeed at getting others to understand our thinking, and (the big payoff) aid us in getting our needs met.

I am willing to bet you have become a master at using synonyms just in the last few years. Your teacher's name was Google (or replace it with the search engine of your choice). We are all quite savvy at digging a little deeper into "wonder what people might call this," as we desperately want the best search results possible. Another way we have succumbed to the lure of synonyms is to go back through a paper we are writing and "spruce it up" a bit with some big words to make it sound more like an A paper than a C paper. Heck, you never know when that might just work! Our push to be understood will quickly turn us into a walking synonym factory. Have you ever caught yourself trying to explain something or ask someone for something and been met with a puzzled look on the other person's face? Immediately, we replay in our heads what we just said, isolate the word(s) we used that might be keeping us from being understood, and then start spitting out synonyms of that word just like we had a form of Thesaurus Tourette's!

The truth is there are some basics you need to understand. You also need to recognize that practice with these types of language relationships (synonyms and antonyms) will make you a stronger writer and reader. The meanings of these terms are as easy as they were when you learned them in elementary school:

- Synonyms—words that mean the same, or almost the same (such as talk and speak)

- Antonyms—words that mean the opposite (such as smile and frown)

- Homonyms—words that are spelled the same and pronounced the same, but have different meanings (table— like where you eat; table—as in water table; table—as in table the conversation)

How you make synonyms, antonyms, and homonyms work for you is where the real impact is felt. These basic word relationships allow us to do very clever things with language. Our most famous and gifted writers make use of every trick of language possible in their writing. Language conventions can achieve many purposes, such as the following:

- Gain appreciation from readers

- Be clever (puns, plays on words, striking contrasts)

- Get the readers' attention

- Shock readers (like a shock jock in print)

- Clarify complex ideas

- Portray deep meaning through exacting language

It might make better sense to "just plain ol' say it" to achieve good, clear communication. There is something to be said for that. The context of the writing is what dictates that. Leaving a note for your parents (or your kids) does not necessitate savvy words to communicate. However, if you are leaving a breakup note for your sig other (please do not do that), then you might labor over it a bit more to be sure that you are expressing exactly the emotion you want the other person to understand.

Another example of the differences in the types of writing we do and the lengths we go to express ourselves might be the contrast between a formal paper for a course and a note to the cable company to express your disparagement over their extravagant charges, as your emolument will not support such a frivolous expenditure of capital, and exact directions for what they can do with their cable service. The point is that when you are going for impact, trying to impress, or fervently need to be understood, using synonyms and antonyms can be very effective.

And as for the title of this chapter, I threw in homonyms because I had to have three things walk into a bar. And because they are cool. Spelled the same . . . pronounced the same . . . do not mean the same thing. Sweet "gotcha."

- **CCSS.ELA-Literacy.CCRA.R.4** Interpret words and phrases as they are used in a text, including determining technical, connotative, and figurative meanings, and analyze how specific word choices shape meaning or tone.

Answers to Word Identification Self-Check on pages 49-51

1. b		**17.** b	
2. c		**18.** gh	
3. c		**19.** l	
4. d		**20.** t	
5. d		**21.** a	
6. b		**22.** c	
7. b		**23.** d	
8. h		**24.** b	
9. b		**25.** a	
10. b		**26.** b	
11. h		**27.** c	
12. l		**28.** b	
13. h		**29.** d	
14. g		**30.** c	
15. k		**31.** a	
16. h		**32.** a	

CPSIA information can be obtained
at www.ICGtesting.com
Printed in the USA
LVOW01s0953220816

501124LV00008B/29/P